WRITERS ON
THE AMERICAN SCREEN

GARLAND REFERENCE LIBRARY
OF THE HUMANITIES
(Vol. 658)

WRITERS ON
THE AMERICAN SCREEN

*A Guide to Film Adaptations
of American and Foreign Literary Works*

Larry Langman

GARLAND PUBLISHING, INC. • NEW YORK & LONDON
1986

Library of Congress Cataloging-in-Publication Data

Langman, Larry.
  Writers on the American screen.

  (Garland reference library of the humanities ;
v. 658)
  Bibliography: p.
  Includes index.
  1. Film adaptations—Bibliography. 2. Moving-
pictures—United States—Bibliography. I. Title.
II. Series.
Z5784.M9L28   1986   016.809   85-28991
[PN1997.85]
ISBN 0-8240-9844-7 (alk. paper)

Cover Design by Bonnie Goldsmith

Printed on acid-free, 250-year-life paper
Manufactured in the United States of America

CONTENTS

PREFACE

The story of the development of the American
film industry would not be complete without a large
portion devoted to those writers whose works have
been adapted to the screen. As basic as this
statement may seem, we tend to take for granted all
those plots and characters that have provided us
with countless hours of viewing pleasure over the
past eighty years, but rarely do we hear or read of
a writer's contribution; it's usually Ford's Grapes
of Wrath or Hawks's To Have and Have Not. Even the
English refer to Olivier's Hamlet, not
Shakespeare's. It is not my intention to diminish
the contributions of others in the depiction of a
literary work, but to recognize and give credit to
the original source of a particular film. The
purpose of this book, therefore, is to present all
the major and many of the minor writers, American
as well as foreign, whose poems, short stories,
plays and novels have been made into motion pictures.

One of the difficulties in compiling such a
collection is in determining which writers to include. I wanted to make the book convenient and
manageable, not a tome. Yet I wished to cite as
many authors as possible, especially those who
would be helpful to researchers, students and
casual readers. Although I set rigid criteria, I
often transgressed because of a certain title or a
particular writer that I believed deserved a place
in this work.

My chief prerequisite was that the work first

had to appear in print. There were and are many talented writers whose stories were created as screenplays and have made excellent films, but they were not the concern of this book. I was interested in literary works which had been adapted to the screen.

My next criterion was relatively simple: to include all those authors who have been recognized by literary critics and historians and are mentioned in such works as Max Herzberg's The Reader's Encyclopedia of American Literature, The Penguin Companion to European Literature and The Oxford Companion to English Literature.

Writers who had some impact on their particular generation were then added. Jack Kerouac is a case in point. Some novels and plays were unique for their time and the film versions considered daring and controversial. Phyllis Bottome's Private Worlds, for example, gave us an early study of the importance of psychiatry in the treatment of the mentally ill. Wednesday's Child, a 1934 film based on a play by Leopold Atlas, revealed the effects of divorce on young children. Elliot Arnold's novel Blood Brother (film version: Broken Arrow) used the western genre to plead for tolerance among races. Mark Reed's play Yes, My Darling Daughter, made into a rather innocuous film in 1939, still retained some of its controversy over a young woman announcing to her parents that she intends to spend a weekend with her fiance. Our final example, The Moon Is Blue, a fatuous film, was steeped in censorship problems in 1947 because of its use of words like "pregnant" and "virgin."

Some writers, admittedly known only within their own genre, were included because of their popularity and because their works have been adapted repeatedly. Thus the reader will find James Oliver Curwood's stories of adventure and action in the Yukon and the Klondike as well as the detective and mystery stories of Earl Derr Biggers, the creator of Charlie Chan.

Other authors, like Carlo Collodi who gave us the lovable character Pinocchio, and Robert Bloch who wrote Psycho, are almost completely unknown, but their works have become famous and widely accepted by the general public. I decided to include them in this collection.

The area of drama, especially its growth in
the United States, is fascinating to trace in terms
of early Hollywood's insatiable appetite for story
material. The film medium affords us the oppor-
tunity to examine the various movements in the
American theater and perhaps to rediscover some of
its more innovative and energetic practitioners.
William Vaughn Moody's The Great Divide as well as
the works of Eugene Walter suggest the stirrings of
realism and modern drama in the first decade of
this century. George S. Kaufman, Ben Hecht and
George Kelly developed the cynical and satirical
farce-comedy to a high art, while Maxwell Anderson
in his Elizabeth the Queen and Winterset attempted
to make poetic drama a permanent fixture on the
stage (all but lost, unfortunately, in their
transfer to the screen). The theater of atmosphere
has been fairly well preserved on film in the works
of such playwrights as Lynn Riggs, Paul Green and
Marc Connelly. Elmer Rice (Street Scene), Clifford
Odets (Golden Boy), Sidney Kingsley (Dead End) and
Lillian Hellman (The Little Foxes) were masters at
creating social realism. Other talented, but now
forgotten, dramatists like Zoe Akins, Rachel
Crothers, Edwin Justin Mayer, Channing Pollock,
Avery Hopwood and John Balderston may deserve a re-
appraisal.
    The American film also gives us the opportu-
nity to revisit many novelists whose works were once
praised by the critics and embraced by a large
segment of the reading public. Among these writers
are Booth Tarkington (the Penrod stories and The
Magnificent Ambersons), John Fox (The Little Shepherd of Kingdom Come), Gene Stratton Porter (A Girl
of the Limberlost), Harold Bell Wright (The Winning
of Barbara Worth) and Helen Hunt Jackson (Ramona).
These writers, and many others listed in these
pages, help us through their works and the films
created from them to witness the changes the novel
has undergone and its different movements -- from
Nineteenth Century romanticism (Cooper and others),
to regionalism as practiced by Edward Eggleston
(The Hoosier Schoolmaster), to realism (Twain), to
naturalism (Hamlin Garland and Frank Norris), to
the proletarian novel (Steinbeck's The Grapes of
Wrath), to the big-city novel (Nelson Algren's The
Man With the Golden Arm), the psychological study,
and so on.

For those interested, this book affords some
curious insights into title changes. For instance,
D.H. Clarke's novel, The Impatient Virgin, was
altered to The Impatient Maiden (1932), in an ob-
vious attempt to fend off the censors who were
challenging Hollywood's abuse of its unwritten
moral code during this period. Conversely, some
titles were made more lurid. Albert Terhune's story, "Driftwood," was transformed into Daring Love
in 1924, while Mildred Cram's stories, "The Beach-
combers" and "Tinfoil," became Sinners in the Sun
and Faithless.

Another worthwhile study would be that of
Hollywood's interpretations of the works of foreign
writers such as Emile Zola, Honore de Balzac,
Flaubert, Tolstoy and Dostoyevski.

Perhaps the most valuable use to which this
book can be put is in helping some brave souls who
wish to undertake a comprehensive study of the
transformation of the written word to the screen.
A less ambitious, but equally important, work would
be an examination of a particular author's writings
and how they have been interpreted by Hollywood.

The book is arranged alphabetically by writer. Each author's works also are listed alphabetically for easy access. When one of these works
has been made into several films, they are entered
chronologically. The film dates are the earliest
release dates and the titles are the ones most
familiar to the general public, although sometimes
they have been changed during re-release. A typi-
cal example is the film "The Devil and Daniel
Webster," based on Stephen Vincent Benet's short
story. Some prints carry the title "All That Money
Can Buy."

The titles in the Index have been sorted by
computer. This may present a minor problem or two
for some users. Titles beginning with "Dr.," for
instance, do not appear amid the "Doctor" listing,
but under their own heading.

I have tried to maintain accuracy in classi-
fying each literary work (novel, play, etc.), but
some writings have appeared only in magazines,
thereby making them difficult to categorize. I
have used the more commonly accepted term "story"
for such entries, regardless of their length.
Finally, no attempt was made to separate nonfiction
works into sub-genres such as memoirs or history,

since in many instances the differentiation became blurred and would prove meaningless.

A work of this nature requires the thoughts and advice of many, especially if it is to be a valuable resource tool. I would like to acknowledge the following people for their assistance: library media consultant Rita Kaikow for her interest and suggestions; Henry Smith and Helene Bell for their ideas; and Spencer Fisher for his editorial help.

SOURCES

Blum, Daniel, ed. Screen World. New York:
    Greenberg, (annual).

Catalog of Copyright Entries: Cumulative Series:
    Motion Pictures. Washington, D.C.: Copyright
    Office, Library of Congress, 1951.

Corliss, Richard. Talking Pictures. New York:
    Penguin Books, 1975.

Everson, William K. American Silent Film. New
    York: Oxford University Press, 1978.

Film Daily Year Book of Motion Pictures (annually).
    New York: Distributed by Arno Press, 1970.

International Motion Picture Almanac (annually).
    New York: Quigley Publishing Company.

Manvell, Roger. Shakespeare and the Film. New
    York: Praeger, 1971.

New York Times Film Reviews (1913-1980). New York:
    Quadrangle Book, Inc.

Willis, John, ed. Screen World. New York: Crown
    Publishers (annually through 1984).

LIST OF DISTRIBUTORS

AA	Allied Artists
AE	Associated Distributors
AFT	American Film Theater
AI	American-International
AJ	Ajax
AMB	Ambassador
APA	A-1 Producers and Distributors
APD	Allied Producers and Distributors
APR	Associated Producers
ART	Artcraft Pictures
ASF	Associated Features
AVCO	Avco-Embassy Corporation
BL	Bluebird
BRA	Brady-World
BV	Buena Vista
C	Cinecom
CBC	Cohen-Brandt-Cohen (Columbia)
CC	Cinema Center
CDI	Continental Distributing, Inc.
CHA	Chadwick Pictures
CHE	Chesterfield Pictures
CLA	Classic Pictures
COF	Continental Distributing, Inc.
COL	Columbia Pictures Corporation
CONN	Conn Pictures
CRC	Cinerama
CUE	Commonwealth United
DAV	Davis Distributing Co.
EDK	Edison-Kleine
EL	Eagle Lion
EQW	Equitable-World
F	Fox Pictures Corp.
FAT	Fine Arts-Triangle
FBO	Film Booking Office
FD	First Division
FN	First National
FP	Famous Pictures
FRO	Frohman

FV	Film Venture
G	Goldwyn Pictures
GRI	Griffith Pictures
HOD	W.W. Hodkinson Co.
IMP	Impact
INC	Ince-Triangle
INS	International Stageplay Pictures
ITC	International Classics
JEN	Jensen Farley
LEM	Levey
LIB	Liberty Pictures
M	Metro
MAB	Arthur Mayer and Joseph Burstyn
MAJ	Majestic Pictures
MAL	Ernst Mattsson
MAS	Mascot Pictures
ME	Merit Pictures
MFR	Continental
MG	Metro-Goldwyn
MGM	Metro-Goldwyn-Mayer
MON	Monogram
MT	Mutual
MTC	Magna Pictures Corp.
NG	National General
NTA	National Television Associates
PAR	Paramount Pictures Corp.
PAT	Pathe
PDC	Producers Distributing Corp.
PRE	Preferred Pictures
PRI	Principal
RB	Rex Beach Productions
RBG	Rex Beach-Goldwyn
REA	Realart
REI	Reliance
REP	Republic Pictures Corp.
RKO	RKO Radio Pictures
SA	Seven Arts
SE	Select Pictures
SEZ	Selznick Studios
SHU	Sherman-United
SR	State Rights
SRO	Selznick Releasing Corp.
TC	Twentieth Century
TCF	Twentieth Century-Fox
THAN	Thanhauser Film Co.
THH	T. Hayes Hunter
TIF	Tiffany Productions
TRI	Triangle Pictures

U	Univeral Pictures
UA	United Artists
UCO	Unique-Fotofilms
UDC	Union Film Distributers
UI	Universal-International
VIC	Victory
VIT	Vitagraph
WB	Warner Brothers
WO	World
WOW	World Wide
WRI	Wright
WW	Sono Art-World Wide

A

ABBEY, EDWARD

Brave Cowboy, The (novel)
    Lonely Are the Brave (1962) U

ABBOTT, GEORGE

Broadway (play in collab. Philip Dunning)
    Broadway (1929) U
    Broadway (1942) U

Coquette (play in collab. Ann Preston)
    Coquette (1929) UA

Damn Yankees (play in collab. Douglass Wallop)
    Damn Yankees (1958) WB

Fall Guy, The (play in collab. James Gleason)
    Fall Guy, The (1930) RKO

Four Walls (play in collab. Dana Burnet)
    Four Walls (1928) MGM
    Straight Is the Way (1934) MGM

Heat Lightning (play in collab. Leon Abrams)
    Heat Lightning (1934) WB
    Highway West (1941) WB

Lilly Turner (play in collab. Philip Dunning)
    Lilly Turner (1933) FN

Love 'Em and Leave 'Em (play in collab. John V.A.
Weaver)
    Love 'Em and Leave 'Em (1926) PAR
    Saturday Night Kid, The (1929) PAR

Three Men on a Horse (play in collab. John C. Holm)

1

Three Men on a Horse (1936) WB

ABRAMS, LEON

Heat Lightning (play in collab. G. Abbott)
    Heat Lightning (1934) WB
    Highway West (1941) WB

ADAMS, FRANK R.

Happiness Preferred (novel)
    Outcast (1937) PAR

Love Piker, The (story in collab. James Fulton)
    Love Piker, The (1923) G

Manhandling Ethel (story)
    Enchantment (1921) PAR

Skin Deep (story)
    Almost a Lady (1926) PDC

ADAMS, SAMUEL HOPKINS

Enter Darcy (story)
    Wanted - a Husband (1919) PAR

Gorgeous Hussy, The (novel)
    Gorgeous Hussy, The (1936) MGM

Harvey Girls, The (novel)
    Harvey Girls, The (1946) MGM

Night Bus (story)
    It Happened One Night (1934) COL
    You Can't Run Away From It (1956) COL

Perfect Specimen, The (novel)
    Perfect Specimen, The (1937) WB

President's Mystery, The (story in collab. with others)
    President's Mystery, The (1936) REP

Siege (novel)

2

        Siege (1925) U

ADDINGTON, SARAH

Bless Their Hearts (story)
    And So They Were Married (1936) COL

Dance Team (novel)
    Dance Team (1932) F

ADE, GEORGE

All Must Marry (story)
    Woman Proof (1923) PAR

College Widow, The (story)
    Freshman Love (1936) WB

County Chairman, The (play)
    County Chairman, The (1936) F

Father and the Boys (story)
    Young As You Feel (1931) F

AGEE, JAMES

Death in the Family, A (novel)
    All the Way Home (1963) PAR

AKINS, ZOE

Daddy's Gone A-Hunting (play)
    Daddy's Gone A-Hunting (1925) MG
    Women Love Once (1931) PAR

Declassee (play)
    Declassee (1925) FN

Furies, The (play)
    Furies, The (1930) FN

Greeks Had a Word for It, The (play)
    Greeks Had a Word for Them, The (1932) UA
    How to Marry a Millionaire (1953) TCF

                        3

Morning Glory (play)
    Morning Glory (1933) RKO
    Stage Struck (1958) RKO

Old Maid, The (play based on Edith Wharton's
novel)
    Old Maid, The (1939) WB

Pardon My Glove (play)
    Ladies Love Brutes (1930) PAR

To You My Life (story)
    Accused (1936) UA

ALBEE, EDWARD

Delicate Balance, A (play)
    Delicate Balance, A (1973) AFT

Who's Afraid of Virginia Woolf? (play)
    Who's Afraid of Virginia Woolf? (1966) WB

ALCOTT, LOUISA M.

Little Men (novel)
    Little Men (1935) MAS
    Little Men (1940) RKO

Little Women (novel)
    Little Women (1919) PAR
    Little Women (1933) RKO
    Little Women (1949) MGM

ALEICHEM, SHOLEM

Tevya (short stories)
    Fiddler on the Roof (1971) UA

ALGREN, NELSON

Man With the Golden Arm, The (novel)
    Man With the Golden Arm, The (1955) UA

Walk on the Wild Side (novel)
    Walk on the Wild Side (1962) COL

ALLEN, FREDERICK LEWIS

Only Yesterday (history)
    Only Yesterday (1933) U

ALLEN, HERVEY

Anthony Adverse (novel)
    Anthony Adverse (1936) WB

ALLEN, JAY PRESSON

First Wife (novel)
    Wives and Lovers (1963) PAR

Just Tell Me What You Want (novel)
    Just Tell Me What You Want (1980) WB

Prime of Miss Jean Brodie, The (play from M.
Spark's novel)
    Prime of Miss Jean Brodie, The (1969) TCF

ALLEN, WOODY

Don't Drink the Water (play)
    Don't Drink the Water (1969) AVCO

Play It Again, Sam (play)
    Play It Again, Sam (1972) PAR

AMBLER, ERIC

Coffin for Dimitrios, A (novel)
    Mask of Dimitrios, The (1944) WB

Journey Into Fear (novel)
    Journey Into Fear (1943) RKO

Light of Day, The (novel)
    Topkapi (1964) UA

5

Uncommon Danger (novel)
    Background to Danger (1943) WB

ANDERSON, EDWARD

Thieves Like Us (novel)
    They Live By Night (1949) RKO
    Thieves Like Us (1974) UA
    Twisted Road, The (1948) RKO

ANDERSON, MAXWELL

Bad Seed, The (play based on William March's
novel)
    Bad Seed, The (1956) WB

Devil's Hornpipe (play in collab. Rouben Mamoulian)
    Never Steal Anything Small (1959) UI

Elizabeth the Queen (play)
    Private Lives of Elizabeth and Essex, The
    (1939) WB

Eve of St. Mark, The (play)
    Eve of St. Mark, The (1944) TCF

Joan of Lorraine (play)
    Joan of Arc (1948) RKO

Key Largo (play)
    Key Largo (1948) WB

Knickerbocker Holiday (play in collab. Kurt Weil)
    Knickerbocker Holiday (1944) UA

Mary of Scotland (play)
    Mary of Scotland (1936) RKO

Saturday's Children (play)
    Saturday's Children (1929) WB
    Maybe It's Love (1935) FN
    Saturday's Children (1940) WB

Washington Merry-Go-Round (novel)
    Washington Merry-Go-Round (1932) COL

What Price Glory (play in collab. L. Stallings)
    What Price Glory (1926) F
    What Price Glory (1952) TCF

Winterset (play)
    Winterset (1936) RKO

ANDERSON, ROBERT

I Never Sang for My Father (play)
    I Never Sang for My Father (1970) COL

Tea and Sympathy (play)
    Tea and Sympathy (1956) MGM

ANDREYEV, LEONID

He Who Gets Slapped (play)
    He Who Gets Slapped (1924) MG

ANET, CLAUDE

Ariane (novel)
    Love in the Afternoon (1957) AA

Mayerling (novel)
    Mayerling (1969) MGM

ANOUIHL, JEAN

Becket (play)
    Becket (1964) PAR

ARLEN, MICHAEL

Ace of Cads, The (short story)
    Ace of Cads, The (1926) PAR

Dancer of Paris, The (short story)
    Dancer of Paris, The (1926) FN

Golden Arrow, The (play)

7

Golden Arrow, The (1936) WB

Green Hat, The (novel)
    Woman of Affairs, A (1929) MGM

ARMSTRONG, PAUL

Alias Jimmy Valentine (play)
    Alias Jimmy Valentine (1920) M
    Alias Jimmy Valentine (1928) MGM

Escape, The (play)
    Escape, The (1928) F

Heart of a Thief, The (play)
    Paths to Paradise (1925) PAR

Heir to the Hurrah, The (play)
    Ever Since Eve (1934) F

Hold That Blonde (play)
    Hold That Blonde (1945) PAR

Romance of the Underworld (play)
    Romance of the Underworld (1929) F

Salomy Jane's Kiss (story in collab. B. Harte)
    Wild Girl (1932) F

ARMSTRONG, WILLIAM H.

Sounder (novel)
    Sounder (1972) TCF

ARNAUD, GEORGE

Wages of Fear, The (novel)
    Sorcerer (1977) PAR

ARNOLD, ELLIOTT

Blood Brothers (novel)
    Broken Arrow (1950) TCF

Commandos (novel)
    First Comes Courage (1943) COL

ASBURY, HERBERT

Gangs of New York (nonfiction)
    Gangs of New York (1938) REP

ASHBROOK, H.

Murder of Stephen Kester, The (novel)
    Green Eyes (1934) CHE

ASHELBE, DETECTIVE

Pepe Le Moko (novel)
    Algiers (1938) UA
    Casbah (1948) UI

ATHERTON, GERTRUDE

Avalanche, The (novel)
    Avalanche, The (1919) ART

Black Oxen (novel)
    Black Oxen (1924) FN

ATLAS, LEOPOLD

Wednesday's Child (play)
    Wednesday's Child (1934) RKO

AUBER

Fra Diavolo (opera)
    Devil's Brother, The (1933) MGM

AUSTEN, JANE

Pride and Prejudice (novel)
    Pride and Prejudice (1940) MGM

9

AXELROD, GEORGE

Goodbye, Charlie (play)
    Goodbye, Charlie (1964) TCF

Seven Year Itch, The (play)
    Seven Year Itch, The (1955) TCF

Will Success Spoil Rock Hunter? (play)
    Will Success Spoil Rock Hunter? (1957) TCF

B

BAGNOLD, ENID

National Velvet (novel)
    National Velvet (1944) MGM

BALDERSTON, JOHN L.

Berkeley Square (play)
    Berkeley Square (1933) F
    I'll Never Forget You (1951) TCF

Dracula (play in collab. Hamilton Deane; from
Bram Stoker's novel)
    Dracula (1931) U

Red Planet Mars (play in collab. John Hoare)
    Red Planet Mars (1952) UA

BALDWIN, FAITH

Apartment for Jenny (story)
    Apartment for Peggy (1948) TCF

Beauty (novel)
    Beauty for Sale (1933) MGM

Comet Over Broadway (short story)
    Comet Over Broadway (1938) WB

Moon's Our Home, The (novel)
    Moon's Our Home, The (1936) PAR

Part-Time Marriage (novel)
    Week-End Marriage (1932) FN

Skyscraper (novel)
    Skyscraper Souls (1932) MGM

Spinster Dinner (novel)
    Love Before Breakfast (1936) U

Wife vs. Secretary (story)
    Wife vs. Secretary (1936) MGM

BALL, JOHN

In the Heat of the Night (novel)
    In the Heat of the Night (1967) UA

BALMER, EDWIN

Dangerous Business (novel)
    Party Girl (1930) TIF

That Royle Girl (novel)
    That Royle Girl (1926) PAR

When Worlds Collide (novel in collab. P. Wylie)
    When Worlds Collide (1952) PAR

BALZAC

Eugenie Grandet (novel)
    Conquering Power, The (1921) M

Honor of the Family (story)
    Honor of the Family (1931) FN

La Duchesse de Langeais (novel)
    Eternal Flame, The (1922) FN

La Peau de Chagrin (novel)
    Slave of Desire (1923) G

Pere Goriot (novel)
　　Paris at Midnight (1926) PDC

BANKS, POLAN

Carriage Entrance (novel)
　　My Forbidden Past (1951) RKO

January Heights (novel)
　　Great Lie, The (1941) WB

Street of Women (novel)
　　Street of Women (1932) WB

BARRETT, WILSON

Sign of the Cross (play)
　　Sign of the Cross (1932) PAR

BARRIE, J.M.

Admirable Crichton, The (play)
　　Male and Female (1919) PAR

Alice Sit by the Fire (play)
　　Darling, How Could You! (1951) PAR

Forever Female (play)
　　Forever Female (1954) PAR

Half an Hour (play)
　　Doctor's Secret, The (1929) PAR

Kiss for Cinderella, A (play)
　　Kiss for Cinderella, A (1926) PAR

Little Minister, The (play)
　　Little Minister, The (1921) VIT
　　Little Minister, The (1934) RKO

Old Lady Shows Her Medals, The (play)
　　Seven Days' Leave (1930) PAR

Peter Pan (play)
　　Peter Pan (1925) PAR

13

Peter Pan (anim. 1953) RKO

Quality Street (play)
    Quality Street (1927) MGM
    Quality Street (1937) RKO

Sentimental Tommy (play)
    Sentimental Tommy (1921) PAR

What Every Woman Knows (play)
    What Every Woman Knows (1934) MGM

BARRY, JULIAN

Lenny (play)
    Lenny (1974) UA

BARRY, PHILIP

Animal Kingdom, The (play)
    Animal Kingdom, The (1932) RKO
    One More Tomorrow (1946) WB

Holiday (play)
    Holiday (1930) PAT
    Holiday (1938) COL

Paris Bound (play)
    Paris Bound (1929) PAT

Philadelphia Story, The (play)
    Philadelphia Story, The (1940) MGM
    High Society (1956) MGM

Spring Dance (play)
    Spring Madness (1938) MGM

Tomorrow and Tomorrow (play)
    Tomorrow and Tomorrow (1932) PAR

Without Love (play)
    Without Love (1945) MGM

You and I (play)
    Bargain, The (1931) FN

BART, JEAN

Man Who Reclaimed His Head, The (play)
    Man Who Reclaimed His Head, The (1935) U

BARTH, JOHN

End of the Road, The (novel)
    End of the Road, The (1970) AA

BAUM, L. FRANK

Wonderful World of Oz, The (novel)
    Wizard of Oz, The (1925) CHA
    Wizard of Oz, The (1939) MGM
    Wiz, The (1978) U

BAUM, VICKI

Grand Hotel (play)
    Grand Hotel (1932) MGM
    Week-End at the Waldorf (1945) MGM

Hotel Berlin (novel)
    Hotel Berlin (1945) WB

Mortgage on Life (novel)
    Woman's Secret, A (1949) RKO

BEACH, LEWIS

Goose Hangs High, The (play)
    Goose Hangs High, The (1925) PAR
    This Reckless Age (1932) PAR

Merry Andrew (play)
    Handy Andy (1934) F
    Young As You Feel (1940) TCF

Square Peg, The (play)
    Denial (925) MG

BEACH, REX

Auction Block, The (novel)
    Auction Block, The (1917) RBG
    Auction Block, The (1926) MGM

Barrier, The (novel)
    Barrier, The (1917) RB
    Barrier, The (1926) MGM
    Barrier, The (1937) PAR

Big Brother (story)
    Big Brother (1923) PAR
    Donovan's Kid (1931) PAR

Brand, The (short story)
    Brand, The (1919) G

Crimson Gardenia, The (novel)
    Crimson Gardenia, The (1918) G

Don Careless (story)
    Avengers, The (1950) REP

Flowing Gold (novel)
    Flowing Gold (1924) FN
    Flowing Gold (1940) WB

Girl From the Outside, The (novel)
    Girl From the Outside, The (1919) G

Goose Woman, The (story)
    Goose Woman, The (1925) U
    Past of Mary Holmes, The (1933) RKO

Iron Trail, The (novel)
    Iron Trail, The (1921) UA

Laughing Bill Hyde (novel)
    Laughing Bill Hyde (1918) G

Mating Call, The (novel)
    Mating Call, The (1928) PAR

Michigan Kid, The (novel)
    Michigan Kid, The (1928) U
    Michigan Kid, The (1947) U

Ne'er-Do-Well, The (novel)
    Ne'er-Do-Well, The (1916) SEL
    Ne'er-Do-Well, The (1923) PAR

Net, The (story)
    Fair Lady (1922) WB

North Wind's Malice, The (story)
    North Wind's Malice, The (1920) G

Recoil, The (short story)
    Recoil, The (1924) MG

Rope's End (novel)
    Sainted Devil, A (1924) PAR

Silver Horde, The (novel)
    Silver Horde, The (1920) G
    Silver Horde, The (1930) RKO

Spoilers, The (novel)
    Spoilers, The (1914)
    Spoilers, The (1923) G
    Spoilers, The (1930) PAR
    Spoilers, The (1942) U
    Spoilers, The (1955) UI

Too Fat to Fight (story)
    Too Fat to Fight (1918) G

BEAGLE, PETER S.

Last Unicorn, The (novel)
    Last Unicorn, The (1982) JEN

BEAUMONT, GERALD

Betty's a Lady (story)
    Count of Ten, The (1928) U

Blue Ribbon, The (story)
    Girl and the Gambler, The (1939) RKO

Dixie (story)
    Dixie Handicap (1925) MG

Even Stephen (story)
    Girl From Coney Island, The (1926) FN

Flower of Napoli (story)
    Man in Blue (1925) U

Frog, The (story)
    Silks and Saddles (1928) U

Gallant Guardsman, The (story)
    My Own Pal (1926) F

Gambling Chaplain, The (story)
    Wild Oats (1926) PDC

Heavenbent (story)
    Rainmaker, The (1926) PAR

Kitten and the King (story)
    Traffic Cop (1926) FBO

Lady Who Played Fidele (story)
    Scarlet Saint (1925) FN

Lord's Referee (story)
    Blue Eagle (1926) F

Money Rider, The (story)
    Down the Stretch (1936) FN

133 at 3 (story)
    133 at 3 (1918) U
    Winner Take All (1932) WB

Said With Soap (story)
    Babe Comes Home (1927) FN

United States Smith (story)
    Pride of the Marines (1936) COL

Winner's Circle (story)
    Reckless Living (1938) U

BEHRMAN, S.N.

Biography (play)
    Biography of a Bachelor Girl (1935) MGM

Brief Moment (play)
    Brief Moment (1933) COL

Jacobowsky and the Colonel (play in collab. F.
Werfel)
    Me and the Colonel (1958) PAR

No Time for Comedy (play)
    No Time for Comedy (1940) WB

Second Man, The (play)
    He Knew Women (1930) RKO

BELASCO, DAVID

Big Fight, The (play)
    Big Fight, The (1930) WW

Case of Becky, The (play)
    Two-Soul Woman, The (1918)

Daddies (play)
    Daddies (1924) WB

DuBarry (play)
    DuBarry, Woman of Passion (1930) UA

Girl of the Golden West, The (play)
    Girl of the Golden West, The (1923) FN
    Girl of the Golden West, The (1930) FN
    Girl of the Golden West, The (1938) MGM

Heart of Maryland, The (play)
    Heart of Maryland, The (1915) VIT

Honorable Mr. Wong, The (story in collab. Achmed
Abdullah)
    Hatchet Man, The (1932) FN

Kiki (play)
    Kiki (1926) FN
    Kiki (1931) UA

Laugh, Clown, Laugh (play in collab. Tom Cushing)
    Laugh, Clown, Laugh (1928) MGM

19

Lord Chumley (play in collab. Henry DeMille)
   Forty Winks (1925) PAR

Men and Women (play in collab. Henry DeMille)
   Men and Women (1925) PAR

Return of Peter Grimm, The (play)
   Return of Peter Grimm, The (1935) RKO

Rose of the Rancho (play in collab. Richard W.
Tully)
   Rose of the Rancho (1936) PAR

Son-Daughter, The (play in collab. George
Scarborough)
   Son-Daughter, The (1933) MGM

Tiger Rose (play)
   Tiger Rose (1923) WB

BELL, THOMAS

All Brides Are Beautiful (story)
   From This Day Forward (1946) RKO

BELLAMAN, HENRY

Kings Row (novel)
   Kings Row (1942) WB

BENCHLEY, PETER

Deep, The (novel)
   Deep, The (1977) COL

Island, The (novel)
   Island, The (1980) U

Jaws (novel)
   Jaws (1975) U

BENET, STEPHEN VINCENT

Devil and Daniel Webster, The (short story)

All That Money Can Buy (1941) RKO

Everybody Was Very Nice (short story)
    Love, Honor and Behave (1938) WB

Famous (short story)
    Just for You (1952) PAR

Sobbin' Women, The (short story)
    Seven Brides for Seven Brothers (1954) MGM

Uriah's Son (short story)
    Necessary Evil (1925) FN

BENNETT, ARNOLD

Book of Carlotta (novel)
    Sacred and Profane Love (1921) PAR

Buried Alive (story)
    His Double Life (1933) PAR
    Holy Matrimony (1943) TCF

BENSON, SALLY

Meet Me in St. Louis (memoirs)
    Meet Me in St. Louis (1944) MGM

BERGER, THOMAS

Little Big Man (novel)
    Little Big Man (1970) CC

BERNSTEIN, CARL

All the President's Men (nonfiction in collab. B.
Woodward)
    All the President's Men (1976) WB

BERNSTEIN, HENRY

Claw, The (play)
    Washington Masquerade, The (1932) MGM

21

BERRIGAN, DANIEL

Trial of the Catonsville Nine, The (play)
    Trial of the Catonsville, Nine, The (1972)
    CINEMA V

BESIER, RUDOLF

Barretts of Wimpole Street, The (play)
    Barretts of Wimpole Street, The (1934) MGM
    Barretts of Wimpole Street, The (1957) MGM

Secrets (play in collab. May Edginton)
    Secrets (1924) FN
    Secrets (1933) UA

BIDDLE, FRANCIS

Mr. Justice Holmes (biography)
    Magnificent Yankee, The (1950) MGM

BIGGERS, EARL DERR

Agony Column, The (novel)
    Second Floor Murder, The (1930) WB
    Passage From Hong Kong (1941) WB

Behind That Curtain (novel)
    Charlie Chan's Chance (1932) F

Black Camel, The (novel)
    Black Camel, The (1931) F

Charlie Chan Carries On (novel)
    Charlie Chan Carries On (1931) F
    Charlie Chan's Murder Cruise (1940) TCF

Charlie Chan's Chance (novel)
    Charlie Chan's Chance (1932) F

Charlie Chan's Greatest Case (novel)
    Charlie Chan's Greatest Case (1933) F

22

Chinese Parrot, The (novel)
    Chinese Parrot, The (1928) U
    Charlie Chan's Courage (1934) F

Deuce of Hearts (novel)
    Take the Stand (1934) LIB

Idle Hands (story)
    Ruling Passion (1916) F
    Millionaire, The (1931) WB
    Way With Women, The (1947) WB

Inside the Lines (play)
    Inside the Lines (1930) RKO

Love Insurance (novel)
    Reckless Age, The (1924) U
    One Night in the Tropics (1940) U

Seven Keys to Baldpate (novel)
    Seven Keys to Baldpate (1917) ART
    Seven Keys to Baldpate (1925) PAR
    Seven Keys to Baldpate (1929) RKO
    Seven Keys to Baldpate (1947) RKO

BIRO, LAJOS

Five Graves to Cairo (play)
    Five Graves to Cairo (1943) PAR

Highwayman, The (play)
    Heart Thief, The (1927) PDC

Hotel Imperial (play)
    Hotel Imperial (1927) PAR
    Hotel Imperial (1939) PAR

Legionary, The (play)
    Silent Lover, The (1926) FN

Royal Scandal, The (play)
    Royal Scandal, The (1945) TCF

BISSON, ALEXANDRE

Madame X (play)

Madame X (1929) MGM
Madame X (1937) MGM
Madame X (1966) U

BLACKMORE, RICHARD D.

Lorna Doone (novel)
Lorna Doone (1923) FN
Lorna Doone (1951) COL

BLATTY WILLIAM PETER

Exorcist, The (novel)
Exorcist, The (1973) WB

BLOCH, ROBERT

Psycho (novel)
Psycho (1960) PAR

Skull of the Marquis de Sade, The (story)
Skull, The (1965) PAR

BOCCACCIO

Tales of the Decameron
Decameron Nights (1953) RKO

BOOTHE, CLARE

Kiss the Boys Goodbye (play)
Kiss the Boys Goodbye (1941) PAR

Margin for Error (play)
Margin for Error (1943) TCF

Women, The (play)
Women, The (1939) MGM
Opposite Sex, The (1956) MGM

BORLAND, HAL

When the Legends Die (novel)
    When the Legends Die (1972) TCF

BOTTOME, PHYLLIS

Danger Signal (novel)
    Danger Signal (1945) WB

Mortal Storm, The (novel)
    Mortal Storm, The (1940) MGM

Private Worlds (novel)
    Private Worlds (1935) PAR

BOULLE, PIERRE

Planet of the Apes (novel)
    Planet of the Apes (19568) TCF

BOYLE, KAY

Maiden, Maiden (short story)
    Five Days of Summer (1982) WB

BRADBURY, RAY

Beast From 20,000 Fathoms, The (short story)
    Beast From 20,000 Fathoms, The (1953) WB

Illustrated Man, The (short stories)
    Illustrated Man, The (1969) WB/SA

Something Wicked This Way Comes (novel)
    Something Wicked This Way Comes (1983) BV

BRAND, MAX

Alcatraz (novel)
    Just Tony (1922) F

Best Bad Man, The (novel)
    Best Bad Man, The (1925) F

Black Rider, The (novel)
    Cavalier, The (1928) TIF

Cuttle's Hired Man (story)
    Against All Odds (1924) F

Dark Rosaleen (story)
    Flying Horseman (1926) F

Destry Rides Again (novel)
    Destry Rides Again (1932) U
    Destry Rides Again (1939) U
    Destry (1955) U

Powder Town (novel)
    Powder Town (1942) RKO

South of the Rio Grande (novel)
    My Outlaw Brother (1951) UA

Trailin' (novel)
    Holy Terror, A (1931) F

Untamed, The (short story)
    Fair Warning (1931) F

BRESLIN, JIMMY

Gang That Couldn't Shoot Straight, The (novel)
    Gang That Couldn't Shoot Straight, The (1971)
    MGM

BREWER, GEORGE

Dark Victory (play)
    Dark Victory (1939) WB
    Stolen Hours (1963) UA

BROADHURST, GEORGE

Bought and Paid For (play)
    Bought and Paid For (1916) BRA
    Bought and Paid For (1922) PAR

Today (play in collab. Abraham Schomer)

Today (1930) MAJ

What Happened to Jones? (play)
    What Happened to Jones? (1925) U

Why Smith Left Home (play)
    Why Smith Left Home (1919) PAR

Wildfire (play in collab. G.V. Hobart)
    Wildfire (1925) VIT

BROMFIELD, LOUIS

Better Than Life (novel)
    It All Came True (1940) WB

Life of Vergie Winters, The (short story)
    Life of Vergie Winters, The (1934) RKO

McLeod's Folly (novel)
    Johnny Come Lately (1943) UA

Modern Hero, A (novel)
    Modern Hero, A (1934) WB

Mrs. Parkington (novel)
    Mrs. Parkington (1944) MGM

Rains Came, The (novel)
    Rains Came, The (1939) TCF
    Rains of Ranchipur, The (1955) TCF

Single Night (story)
    Night After Night (1932) PAR

Twenty-Four Hours (novel)
    Twenty-Four Hours (1931) PAR

BRONTE, CHARLOTTE

Jane Eyre (novel)
    Jane Eyre (1921) HOD
    Jane Eyre (1934) MON
    Jane Eyre (1944) TCF

BRONTE, EMILY

Wuthering Heights (novel)
    Wuthering Heights (1939) UA

BROWN, JOE DAVID

Addie Pray (novel)
    Paper Moon (1973) PAR

BROWN, MARTIN

Cobra (play)
    Cobra (1925) PAR

Exciters, The (play)
    Exciters, The (1923) PAR

Great Music (play)
    Soul Fire (1925) FN

Idol, The (play)
    Mad Genius, The (1931) WB

Lady, The (play)
    Lady, The (1925) FN
    Secret of Madame Blanche, The (1933) MGM

Paris (play)
    Paris (1929) FN

BRUSH, KATHARINE

Glitter (story)
    Drop Kick (1927) FN

Marry for Money (story)
    Mannequin (1938) MGM

Night Club (novel)
    Night Club (1929) PAR

Red Headed Woman (novel)
    Red Headed Woman (1932) MGM

Young Man of Manhattan (novel)
    Young Man of Manhattan (1930) PAR

BUCHWALD, ART

Gift From the Boys, A (novel)
    Surprise Package (1960) COL

BUCK, PEARL S.

China Sky (novel)
    China Sky (1945) RKO

Dragon Seed (novel)
    Dragon Seed (1944) MGM

Good Earth, The (novel)
    Good Earth, The (1937) MGM

Satan Never Sleeps (novel)
    Satan Never Sleeps (1962) TCF

BULWER-LYTTON, SIR EDWARD

Cardinal Richelieu (play)
    Cardinal Richelieu (1935) TC

Lady of Lyons, The (play)
    In the Name of Love (1925) PAR

Last Days of Pompeii, The (novel)
    Last Days of Pompeii, The (1935) RKO

BURDICK, EUGENE

Fail-Safe (novel in collab. Harvey Wheeler)
    Fail-Safe (1964) COL

BURKE, THOMAS

Chink and the Child, The (short story)
    Broken Blossoms (1919) GRI

Twinkletoes (short story)
    Twinkletoes (1927) FN

BURNETT, FRANCES HODGSON

Dawn of a Tomorrow, The (play, novel)
    Dawn of a Tomorrow, The (1924) PAR

Editha's Burglar (story)
    Family Secret (1924) U

Fantasy, The (novel)
    Little Princess, The (1917) ART
    Little Princess, The (1939) TCF

Little Lord Fauntleroy (novel)
    Little Lord Fauntleroy (1915)
    Little Lord Fauntleroy (1921) UA
    Little Lord Fauntleroy (1936) UA

Louisiana (novel)
    Louisiana (1919)

That Lass O'Lowries (story)
    Flame of Life (1923) U

BURNETT, W.R.

Across the Aisle (story)
    36 Hours to Kill (1936) F

Adobe Walls (novel)
    Arrowhead (1953) PAR

Cool Breeze (novel)
    Cool Breeze (1972) MGM

Dark Hazard (novel)
    Dark Hazard (1934) FN

High Sierra (novel)
    High Sierra (1941) WB
    Colorado Territory (1949) WB
    I Died a Thousand Times (1955) WB

Iron Man (story)
    Some Blondes Are Dangerous (1937) U

Little Caesar (novel)
    Little Caesar (1930) WB

Saint Johnson (story)
    Law and Order (1932) U

Vanity Row (novel)

Accused of Murder (1956) REP

BURNS, WALTER NOBLE

Robin Hood of El Dorado, The (biography)
    Robin Hood of El Dorado (1936) MGM

Saga of Billy the Kid (biography)
    Billy the Kid (1930) MGM
    Billy the Kid (1941) MGM

BURROUGHS, EDGAR RICE

Land That Time Forgot, The (novel)
    Land That Time Forgot, The (1975) AI

People That Time Forgot, The (novel)
    People That Time Forgot, The (1977) AI

Tarzan of the Apes (novel)
    Tarzan of the Apes (1918) FN
    Tarzan, the Ape Man (1932) MGM

Tarzan, the Fearless (story)
    Tarzan, the Fearless (1933) PRI

BURROWS, ABE

Can-Can (play)
    Can-Can (1960) TCF

BUSCH, NIVEN

Duel in the Sun (novel)
    Duel in the Sun (1946) SEZ

Furies, The (novel)
    Furies, The (1950) PAR

They Dream of Home (novel)
    Till the End of Time (1946) RKO

We the O'Learys (story)
    In Old Chicago (1938) TCF

31

C

CAIN, JAMES M.

Baby in the Icebox, The (story)
    She Made Her Bed (1934) PAR

Butterfly (novel)
    Butterfly (1982) ANALYSIS

Double Indemnity (novel)
    Double Indemnity (1944) PAR

Love's Lovely Counterfeit (story)
    Slightly Scarlet (1956) RKO

Mildred Pierce (novel)
    Mildred Pierce (1945) WB

Modern Cinderella (novel)
    When Tomorrow Comes (1939) U

Postman Always Rings Twice, The (novel)
    Postman Always Rings Twice, The (1946) MGM
    Postman Always Rings Twice, The (1981) PAR

Serenade (novel)
    Serenade (1956) WB

Wife, Husband and Friend (novel)
    Wife, Husband and Friend (1939) TCF

CAINE, HALL

Barbed Wire (novel)
    Barbed Wire (1927) PAR

Christian, The (novel)
    Christian, The (1923) VIT

Eternal City, The (novel)
    Eternal City, The (1915) FP
    Eternal City, The (1923) FN

Master of Man (novel)
    Name the Man (1924) MG

Woman of the Knockaloe (novel)
    Barbed Wire (1927) PAR

Woman Thou Gavest Me, The (novel)
    Woman Thou Gavest Me, The (1919) PAR

CALDWELL, ERSKINE

Claudelle Inglish (novel)
    Claudelle Inglish (1961) WB

God's Little Acre (novel)
    God's Little Acre (1958) UA

Tobacco Road (novel; play version by Jack Kirkland)
    Tobacco Road (1941) TCF

CAMPBELL, JOHN W.

Who Goes There? (short story)
    Thing, The (1951) RKO
    Thing, The (1982) U

CANNING, VICTOR

Castle Minerva (novel)
    Masquerade (1965) UA

House of the Seven Flies, The (story)
    House of the Seven Hawks, The (1959) MGM

Panther's Moon (novel)
    Spy Hunt (1950) UI

Rainbird Pattern (novel)
    Family Plot (1976) U

Venetian Bird (novel)
    Assassin, The (1953) UA

CAPOTE, TRUMAN

Among the Paths to Eden (short story)
    Trilogy (1969) AA

Breakfast at Tiffany's (novel)
    Breakfast at Tiffany's (1961) PAR

Christmas Memory, A (short story)
    Trilogy (1969) AA

In Cold Blood (novel)
    In Cold Blood (1967) COL

Miriam (short story)
    Trilogy (1969) AA

CARLETON, WILL

Over the Hill to the Poor House (poem)
    Over the Hill (1917) PAT
    Over the Hill (1931) F

CARPENTER, EDWARD CHILDS

Bachelor Father, The (play)
    Bachelor Father, The (1931) MGM

Cinderella Man, The (play)
    Cinderella Man, The (1917) G

Code of Victor Jallot, The (story)
    Love Mart, The (1927) FN

Connie Goes Home (story)
    Major and the Minor, The (1942) PAR

Order, Please (story)
    One New York Night (1935) MGM

Perfect Gentleman, The (play)
    Perfect Gentleman, The (1935) MGM

Three Bears (story)
    Three Men and a Girl (1919) PAR

Whistling in the Dark (play in collab. Laurence Gross)
    Whistling in the Dark (1933) MGM
    Whistling in the Dark (1941) MGM

CARR, JOHN DICKSON

Emperor's Snuffbox, The (novel)
    City After Midnight (1959) RKO

Gentleman From Paris (novel)
    Man With a Cloak (1951) MGM

CARROLL, LEWIS

Alice's Adventures in Wonderland (novel)
    Alice in Wonderland (1927) PAT
    Alice in Wonderland (1931) UCO
    Alice in Wonderland (1933) PAR
    Alice in Wonderland (anim. 1951) RKO

CARSON, RACHEL L.

Sea Around Us, The (nonfiction)
    Sea Around Us, The (1953) RKO

CARSON, ROBERT

Come Be My Love (novel)
    Once More, My Darling (1949) U

35

It Happened in Hollywood (story in collab. William
Wellman)
    Star Is Born, A (1937) UA
    Star Is Born, A (1954) WB
    Star Is Born, A (1976) WB

Legal Bride (short story)
    Groom Wore Spurs, The (1951) UI

Third Girl From the Right (story)
    Ain't Misbehavin' (1955) U

CASPARY, VERA

Blind Mice (story in collab. Winifred Lenihan)
    Working Girls (1931) PAR

Laura (novel)
    Laura (1944) TCF

Odd Thursday (story)
    Such Women Are Dangerous (1934) F

Suburbs (short story)
    Night of June 13th, The (1932) PAR

CATHER, WILLA

Lost Lady, A (novel)
    Lost Lady, A (1925) WB
    Lost Lady, A (1934) FN

CATTO, MAX

Devil at 4 O'Clock, The (novel)
    Devil at 4 O'Clock, The (1961) COL

Fire Down Below (novel)
    Fire Down Below (1957) COL

Killing Frost, The (novel)
    Trapeze (1956) UA

Mister Moses (novel)
    Mister Moses (1965) UA

Prize of Gold, A (novel)
    Prize of Gold, A (1955) COL

Seven Thieves (novel)
    Seven Thieves (1960) TCF

CERAM, C.W.

Gods, Graves and Scholars (nonfiction)
    Valley of the Kings (1954) MGM

CERVANTES, MIGUEL DE

Don Quixote (novel)
    Don Quixote (1915) PAT
    Man of La Mancha (1972) UA

CHAMBERS, ROBERT W.

Between Friends (novel)
    Between Friends (1924) VIT

Cardigan (novel)
    Cardigan (1922) AR

Common Law, The (novel)
    Common Law, The (1923) SEZ
    Common Law, The (1931) RKO

Danger Mark, The (novel)
    Danger Mark, The (1918) ART

Girl Philippa, The (novel)
    Girl Philippa, The (1917) VIT

Husbands of Edith (novel)
    Fast Worker (1924) U

Firing Line, The (novel)
    Firing Line, The (1919) PAR

Operator 13 (stories)
    Operator 13 (1934) MGM

Restless Sex, The (novel)
    Restless Sex, The (1920) PAR

CHAMBERS, WHITMAN

Campinile Murders, The (novel)
    Murder on the Campus (1934) CHE

Come On, The (novel)
    Come On, The (1956) AA

Murder for a Wanton (novel)
    Sinner Take All (1937) MGM

CHANDLER, RAYMOND

Big Sleep, The (novel)
    Big Sleep, The (1946) WB

Farewell, My Lovely (novel)
    Falcon Takes Over, The (1942)
    Murder, My Sweet (1945) RKO
    Farewell, My Lovely (1975) AVCO

High Window, The (novel)
    Time to Kill (1942) TCF
    Brasher Doubloon, The (1947) TCF

Lady in the Lake (novel)
    Lady in the Lake (1947) MGM

Little Sister, The (novel)
    Marlowe (1969) MGM

Long Goodbye, The (novel)
    Long Goodbye, The (1973) UA

CHARTERIS, LESLIE

Angel of Doom (novel)
    Saint Strikes Back, The (1939) RKO

Meet the Tiger (novel)

Saint Meets the Tiger, The (1943) REP

Million Pound Day, The (story)
    Saint in London, The (1939) RKO

Saint in New York, The (novel)
    Saint in New York, The (1938) RKO

CHASE, BORDEN

Chisholm Trail, The (story)
    Red River (1948) UA

Concerto (story)
    I've Always Loved You (1946) REP

Hell's Kitchen Has a Pantry (story)
    Devil's Party, The (1938) U

Pay to Learn (story)
    Navy Comes Through, The (1942) RKO

CHASE, JAMES HADLEY

I'll Get You for This (novel)
    Lucky Nick Cain (1951) TCF

World in My Pocket (novel)
    World in My Pocket (1962) MGM

CHASE, MARY C.

Bernardine (play)
    Bernardine (1957) TCF

Harvey (play)
    Harvey (1950) UI

CHAYEFSKY, PADDY

Altered States (novel)
    Altered States (1980) WB

Middle of the Night (play)

Middle of the Night (1959) COL

CHEEVER, JOHN

Swimmer, The (short story)
    Swimmer, The (1968) COL

CHEKHOV, ANTON

Shooting Party, The (short story)
    Summer Storm (1944) UA

Three Sisters, The (play)
    Three Sisters, The (1977) NTA

CHRISTIE, AGATHA

A.B.C. Murders, The (novel)
    Alphabet Murders, The (1966) MGM

And Then There Were None (novel)
    And Then There Were None (1945) TCF

Love From a Stranger (short story)
    Love From a Stranger (1937) UA

Witness for the Prosecution (play)
    Witness for the Prosecution (1958) UA

CHURCHILL, WINSTON

Second World War, The (nonfiction)
    Finest Hours, The (1964) COL

CLARK, BRIAN

Whose Life Is It Anyway? (play)
    Whose Life Is It Anyway? (1981) MGM

CLARK, WALTER VAN TILBURG

Ox-Bow Incident, The (novel)

Ox-Bow Incident, The (1943) TCF

Track of the Cat (novel)
    Track of the Cat (1954) WB

CLARKE, DONALD HENDERSON

Impatient Virgin, The (novel)
    Impatient Maiden, The (1922) U

Louis Beretti (novel)
    Born Reckless (1930) F

CLORK, HARRY

Milky Way, The (play in collab. L. Root)
    Milky Way, The (1936) PAR
    Kid From Brooklyn, The (1946) RKO

See My Lawyer (play in collab. R. Maibaum)
    See My Lawyer (1945) U

COHAN, GEORGE M.

Broadway Jones (play)
    Broadway Jones (1917) ART

Gambling (play)
    Gambling (1934) F

Get-Rich-Quick Wallingford (play)
    Get-Rich-Quick Wallingford (1921) PAR

Home Towners, The (play)
    Home Towners, The (1928) WB
    Times Square Playboy (1936) WB
    Ladies Must Live (1940) WB

Hurry Kane (play in collab. R. Lardner)
    Fast Company (1929) PAR

Little Johnny Jones (play)
    Little Johnny Jones (1923) WF

Little Nellie Kelly (play)

Little Nellie Kelly (1940) MGM

Miracle Man, The (play from F.L. Packard's novel)
    Miracle Man, The (1919) PAR

Seven Keys to Baldpate (play from E.D. Biggers' novel)
    Seven Keys to Baldpate (1925) PAR
    Seven Keys to Baldpate (1929) RKO

Song and Dance Man, The (play)
    Song and Dance Man, The (1926) PAR
    Song and Dance Man, The (1936) TCF

COLETTE

Gigi (novel)
    Gigi (1958) MGM

COLLIER, WILLIAM

Hottentot, The (play)
    Hottentot, The (1922) FN
    Hottentot, The (1929) WB
    Going Places (1939) WB

COLLINS, WILKIE

Moonstone, The (novel)
    Moonstone, The (1934) MON

Woman in White, The (novel)
    Woman in White, The (1948) WB

COLLISON, WILSON

Blonde Baby (story)
    Three Wise Girls (1932) COL

Congo Landing (story)
    Congo Maisie (1940)

Crusader, The (play)
    Crusader, The (1932) MAJ

Getting Gertie's Garter (play in collab. A. Hopwood)
    Getting Gertie's Garter (1927) PDC
    Getting Gertie's Garter (1946) UA

Girl in Upper C (story)
    Girl in the Pullman (1927) PAT

Maisie (novel)
    Maisie (1939) MGM

Passionate Sonata (novel)
    Expensive Women (1931) FN

Red Dust (play)
    Red Dust (1932) MGM
    Mogambo (1953) MGM

Red-Haired Alibi (novel)
    Red-Haired Alibi (1932) TOWER

Sing Sinner Sing (play)
    Sing Sinner Sing (1933) MAJ

There's Always a Woman (story)
    There's Always a Woman (1938) COL

Up in Mabel's Room (play in collab. Otto Harbach)
    Up in Mabel's Room (1944) UA

COLLODI, CARLO

Pinocchio (fairy tale)
    Pinocchio (anim. 1940) RKO

CONDON, RICHARD

Manchurian Candidate, The (novel)
    Manchurian Candidate, The (1962) UA

Oldest Profession, The (novel)
    Happy Thieves, The (1962) UA

Winter Kills (novel)
    Winter Kills (1979) AVCO

CONNELL, RICHARD

Friend of Napoleon, A (story)
    Seven Faces (1929) F

Little Bit of Broadway, A (short story)
    Bright Lights (1925) MG

Most Dangerous Game, The (short story)
    Most Dangerous Game, The (1932) RKO
    Game of Death, A (1945) RKO
    Run for the Sun (1956) UA

Not Damaged (short story)
    Not Damaged (1930) F

One Hundred Dollars (short story)
    New Year's Eve (1929) F

Pat and Mike (short story)
    Bullets for O'Hara (1941) WB

Where Is the Tropic of Capricorn? (short story)
    East of Broadway (1924) AE

CONNELLY, MARC

Beggar on Horseback (play in collab. G.S. Kaufman)
    Beggar on Horseback (1925) PAR

Dulcy (play in collab. G.S. Kaufman)
    Dulcy (1923) FN
    Not So Dumb (1930) MGM
    Not So Dumb (1940) MGM

Farmer Takes a Wife, The (play in collab. Frank
Elser)
    Farmer Takes a Wife, The (1935) F
    Farmer Takes a Wife, The (1953) TCF

Green Pastures, The (play)
    Green Pastures, The (1936) WB

Merton of the Movies (play in collab. G.S. Kaufman)
    Merton of the Movies (1924) PAR

44

Merton of the Movies (1947) MGM

To the Ladies (play in collab. G.S. Kaufman)
    To the Ladies (1923) PAR

CONNOR, RALPH

Sky Pilot, The (novel)
    Sky Pilot, The (1921) FN

CONRAD, JOSEPH

Because of the Dollars (story)
    Laughing Anne (1954) REP

Lord Jim (novel)
    Lord Jim (1925) PAR
    Lord Jim (1965) COL

Nostromo (novel)
    Silver Treasure (1926) F

Rescue, The (story)
    Rescue, The (1929) UA

Romance (story)
    Road to Romance, The (1927) MGM

Secret Sharer, The (short story)
    Face to Face (1952) RKO

Victory (novel)
    Victory (1919) PAR
    Dangerous Paradise (1930) PAR
    Victory (1940) PAR

CONROY, PAT

Lords of Discipline, The (novel)
    Lords of Discipline, The (1983) PAR

Water Is Wide, The (novel)
    Conrack (1974) TCF

COOPER, JAMES FENIMORE

Last of the Mohicans, The (novel)
      Last of the Mohicans, The (1920) APR
      Last of the Mohicans, The (1936) UA
      Last of the Redmen (1947) COL

Leatherstocking Tales, The (novels)
      Iroquois Trail, The (1950) UA

CORMAN, AVERY

Kramer vs. Kramer (novel)
      Kramer vs. Kramer (1979) COL

CORMIER, ROBERT

I Am the Cheese (novel)
      I Am the Cheese (1983) ALMI

CORWIN, NORMAN

My Client Curley (story)
      Once Upon a Time (1944) COL

COSTAIN, THOMAS B.

Black Rose, The (novel)
      Black Rose, The (1950) TCF

Silver Chalice, The (novel)
      Silver Chalice, The (1954) WB

COWARD, NOEL

Bitter Sweet (play)
      Bitter Sweet (1940) MGM

Cavalcade (play)
      Cavalcade (1933) F

Design for Living (play)
      Design for Living (1933) PAR

Private Lives (play)
    Private Lives (1931) MGM

Queen Was in the Parlor, The (play)
    Tonight Is Ours (1933) PAR

Tonight at 8:30 (play)
    We Were Dancing (1942) MGM

COWEN, RON

Summertree (play)
    Summertree (1971) COL

COZZENS, JAMES GOULD

By Love Possessed (novel)
    By Love Possessed (1961) UA

Last Adam, The (novel)
    Doctor Bull (1933) F

CRAM, MILDRED

Beachcomber, The (story)
    Sinners in the Sun (1932) PAR

Girls Together (story)
    This Modern Age (931) MGM

Sadie of the Desert (story)
    Subway Sadie (1926) (1926) FN

Scotch Valley (story)
    Amateur Daddy (1932) F

Thin Air (story)
    Stars Over Broadway (1935) WB

Tinfoil (story)
    Faithless (1932) MGM

Wings Over Honolulu (story)
    Wings Over Honolulu (1937) U

CRANE, STEPHEN

Bride Comes to Yellow Sky, The (short story)
    Face to Face (1952) RKO

Monster, The (story)
    Face of Fire (1959) AA

Red Badge of Courage, The (novel)
    Red Badge of Courage, The (1951) MGM

CRAVEN, FRANK

First Year, The (play)
    First Year, The (1926) F
    First Year, The (1932) F

New Brooms (play)
    New Brooms (1925) PAR

Salt Water (play in collab. with others)
    Her First Mate (1933) U

Too Many Crooks (play)
    Too Many Crooks (1931) RKO

CRAWFORD, CHRISTINA

Mommie Dearest (biography)
    Mommie Dearest (1981) PAR

CRICHTON, MICHAEL

Andromeda Strain, The (novel)
    Andromeda Strain, The (1971) U

Terminal Man, The (novel)
    Terminal Man, The (1974) WB

CRICHTON, ROBERT

Secret of Santa Vittoria, The (novel)

Secret of Santa Vittoria, The ((1969) UA

CROISSET, FRANCIS de

Arsene Lupin (play in collab. Maurice Le Blanc)
    Arsene Lupin (1932) MGM

Il Etait Une Fois (play)
    Woman's Face, A (1941) MGM

La Passerella (play in collab. Fred De Gresac)
    Marriage of Kitty, The (1915) PAR
    Afraid to Love (1927) PAR

CRONIN, A.J.

Grand Canary (novel)
    Grand Canary (1934) Lasky/F

Green Years, The (novel)
    Green Years, The (1946) MGM

Jupiter Laughs (play)
    Shining Victory (1941) WB

Kaleidoscopescope in K (story)
    Once to Every Woman (1934) PAR

Keys of the Kingdom, The (novel)
    Keys of the Kingdom, The (1944) TCF

Vigil in the Night (novel)
    Vigil in the Night (1940) RKO

CROTHERS, RACHEL

As Husbands Go (play)
    As Husbands Go (1934) F

Little Journey, A (play)
    Little Journey, A (1927) MGM

Mary the Third (play)
    Wine of Youth (1924) MG

Mother Carey's Chickens (play in collab. K.D. Wiggin)
        Mother Carey's Chickens (1938) RKO

Old Lady 31 (play)
        Old Lady 31 (1920) M

Susan and God (play)
        Susan and God (1940) MGM

When Ladies Meet (play)
        When Ladies Meet (1933) MGM
        When Ladies Meet (1941) MGM

CROWLEY, MART

Boys in the Band, The (play)
        Boys in the Band, The (1970) NG

CUNNINGHAM, JOHN W.

Tin Star, The (story)
        High Noon (1952) UA

CURWOOD, JAMES OLIVER

Alaskan, The (novel)
        Alaskan, The (1924) PAR

Back to God's Country (story)
        Back to God's Country (1919) FN
        Back to God's Country (1927) U
        Back to God's Country (1953) U

Baree, Son of Kazan (short story)
        Baree, Son of Kazan (1918) VIT
        Baree, Son of Kazan (1925) VIT

Caryl of the Mountains (novel)
        Trails of the Wild (1935) AMB

Country Beyond, The (novel)
        Country Beyond, The (1926) F
        Country Beyond, The (1936) TCF

Fangs of the North (novel)
    Call of the Klondike (1950) MON

Flaming Forest, The (story)
    Flaming Forest, The (1926) MGM

Four Minutes Late (story)
    Northern Frontier (1935) AMB

Girl Who Dared, The (novel)
    Paid in Advance (1919) U

God's Country and the Woman (novel)
    God's Country and the Woman (1916) VIT
    God's Country and the Woman (1937) WB

Cold Hunters, The (novel)
    Trail of the Yukon (1949) MON
    Yukon Gold (1952) MON

Golden Snare, The (novel)
    Golden Snare, The (1921) FN

Isobel, or the Trail's End (novel)
    Isobel, or the Trail's End (1920) DAV

Nomads of the North (novel)
    Nikki, Wild Dog of the North (1961) BV

Northern Trail, The (short story)
    Northern Trail, The (1921)

Playing With Fire (story)
    Song of the Trail (1936) AMB

Quest of Joan, The (story)
    Prisoners of the Storm (1926) U

Retribution (story)
    Timber Fury (1950) EL

River's End, The (novel)
    River's End, The (1920) FN
    River's End, The (1931) WB
    River's End, The (1940) WB

Steele of the Royal Mounted (story)
    Steele of the Royal Mounted (1925) VIT

Swift Lightning (novel)
    Call of the Yukon (1938) REP

Tentacles of the North (story)
    Snow Dog (1950) MON

Wheels of Fate (novel)
    Code of the Mounted (1935) AMB

Wolf Hunters (novel)
    Trail Beyond, The (1934) MON

D

DAHL, ROALD

Charlie and the Chocolate Factory (novel)
    Willy Wonka & the Chocolate Factory (1971) PAR

DANA, RICHARD HENRY

Two Years Before the Mast (novel)
    Two Years Before the Mast (1946) PAR

DANE CLEMENCE

Bill of Divorcement, A (play)
    Bill of Divorcement, A (1932) RKO
    Bill of Divorcement, A (1940) RKO

St. Martin's Lane (play)
    Sidewalks of London (1940) PAR

DAUDET, ALPHONSE

Kings in Exile (novel)
    Confessions of a Queen (1925) MG

DAVENPORT, MARCIA

East Side, West Side (novel)
    East Side, West Side (1949) MGM

Valley of Decision, The (novel)
    Valley of Decision, The (1945) MGM

DAVIES, HUBERT HENRY

Girl From Tenth Avenue, The (play)
    Girl From Tenth Avenue, The (1935) WB

Strictly Modern (play)
    Strictly Modern (1930) FN

DAVIS, ELMER

Friends of Mr. Sweeney (novel)
    Friends of Mr. Sweeney (1934) WB

I'll Show You the Town (novel)
    I'll Show You the Town (1925) U

DAVIS, OSSIE

Purlie Victorious (play)
    Gone Are the Days (1963) HAMMER

DAVIS, OWEN

At Yale (story)
    Hold 'Em Yale (1928) PAT

Broadway After Dark (play)
    Broadway After Dark (1924) WB

Donovan Affair, The (play)
    Donovan Affair, The (1929) COL

Easy Come, Easy Go (play)
    Easy Come, Easy Go (1928) PAR
    Easy Come, Easy Go (1947) PAR

Easy Money (play)

Only Saps Work (1930) PAR

Eternal Grind, The (play)
        Eternal Grind, The (1916) VIT

Forever After (play)
        Forever After (1926) FN

Great Gatsby, The (play from Fitzgerald's novel)
        Great Gatsby, The (1949) PAR

Haunted House, The (play)
        Haunted House, The (1928) FN

Icebound (play)
        Icebound (1924) PAR

Jezebel (play)
        Jezebel (1938) WB

Lighthouse by the Sea, The (play)
        Lighthouse by the Sea, The (1925) WB

Mr. and Mrs. North (play)
        Mr. and Mrs. North (1942) MGM

Nellie, the Beautiful Cloak Model (play)
        Nellie, the Beautiful Cloak Model (1924) MG

Nervous Wreck, The (play)
        Nervous Wreck, The (1926) PDC
        Whoopie (1930) UA
        Up in Arms (1944) RKO

Ninth Guest, The (play)
        Ninth Guest, The (1934) COL

Tonight at Twelve (play)
        Tonight at Twelve (1929) U

Up the Ladder (play)
        Up the Ladder (1925) U

DAVIS, RICHARD HARDING

Bar Sinister, The (story)
        Almost Human (1927) PAT

It's a Dog's Life (1955) MGM

Dictator, The (novel, play)
    Dictator, The (1922) PAR

Exiles (story)
    Fugitives (1929) F

Gallagher (novel)
    Let 'Er Go, Gallagher (1928) PAT

Grand Cross of the Crescent, The (novel)
    Stephen Steps Out (1923) PAR

Ranson's Folly (story)
    Ranson's Folly (1926) FN

Soldiers of Fortune (novel)
    Soldiers of Fortune (1919) HOD

DE HARTOG, JAN

Four Poster, The (play)
    Four Poster, The (1952) COL

Inspector, The (novel)
    Lisa (1962) TCF

Little Ark, The (novel)
    Little Ark, The (1972) NG

Stella (story)
    Key, The (1958) COL

DE LA RAMEE, LOUISE

Dog of Flanders, A (novel)
    Boy of Flanders (1924) MG
    Dog of Flanders, A (1935) RKO

DE VOTO, BERNARD

Across the Wide Missouri (nonfiction)
    Across the Wide Missouri (1951) MGM

DE VRIES, PETER

Reuben, Reuben (novel)
    Reuben, Reuben (1983) TCF

Witch's Milk (novella)
    Pete 'n' Tillie (1972) U

DE WAHL, LOUIS

Joyful Beggar (novel)
    Francis of Assisi (1961) TCF

DEFOE, DANIEL

Amorous Adventures of Moll Flanders, The (novel)
    Amorous Adventures of Moll Flanders, The
    (1965) PAR

Robinson Crusoe (novel)
    Robinson Crusoe on Mars (1964) PAR

DELL FLOYD

Bachelor Father (novel)
    Casanova Brown (1944) RKO

DEVAL, JACQUES

Her Cardboard Lover (play)
    Her Cardboard Lover (1942) MGM

Journal of a Crime (play)
    Journal of a Crime (1934) FN

Marie Galante (novel)
    Marie Galante (1934) F

Miss Tatlock's Millions (play)
    Miss Tatlock's Millions (1948) PAR

Say It in French (play)
    Say It in French (1938) PAR

Tovarich (play)
    Tovarich (1937) WB

DICK, PHILIP K.

Do Androids Dream of Electric Sheep? (novel)
    Blade Runner (1982) WB

DICKENS, CHARLES

Christmas Carol, A (story)
    Christmas Carol, A (1938) MGM

David Copperfield (novel)
    David Copperfield (1935) U

Dombey and Son (novel)
    Dombey and Son (1919) TRI
    Rich Man's Folly (1931) PAR

Great Expectations (novel)
    Great Expectations (1916) PAR
    Great Expectations (1934) U

Mystery of Edwin Drood, The (novel)
    Mystery of Edwin Drood, The (1935) U

Oliver Twist (novel)
    Oliver Twist (1916) PAR
    Oliver Twist (1922) FN
    Oliver Twist (1933) MON

Tale of Two Cities, A (novel)
    Tale of Two Cities, A (1916) F
    Only Way, The (1926) UA
    Tale of Two Cities, A (1935) MGM

DICKEY, JAMES

Deliverance (novel)
    Deliverance (1972) WB

DIXON, THOMAS

Clansman, The (novel)
    Birth of a Nation, The (1915) UA

DOCTOROW, E.L.

Book of Daniel, The (novel)
    Daniel (1983) PAR

Ragtime (novel)
    Ragtime (1981) PAR

Welcome to Hard Times (novel)
    Welcome to Hard Times (1967) MGM

DOSTOYEVSKI, FYODOR

Brothers Karamazov, The (novel)
    Brothers Karamazov, The (1958) MGM

Crime and Punishment (novel)
    Crime and Punishment (1935) COL
    Crime and Punishment, U.S.A. (1959) AA

DOUGLAS, LLOYD C.

Big Fisherman, The (novel)
    Big Fisherman, The (1959) BV

Disputed Passage (novel)
    Disputed Passage (1939) PAR

Green Light (novel)
    Green Light (1937) WB

Magnificent Obsession (novel)
    Magnificent Obsession (1935) U
    Magnificent Obsession (1954) UI

Robe, The (novel)
    Robe, The (1953) TCF

White Banners (novel)
    White Banners (1938) WB

DOYLE, A. CONAN

Adventure of the Dancing Men, The (short story)
    Sherlock Holmes and the Secret Weapon (1942) U

Adventure of the Dying Detective, The (short story)
    Return of Sherlock Holmes, The (1929) PAR

Adventures of Brigadier Gerard, The (short stories)
    Fighting Eagle, The (1917) PAT

His Last Bow (short story)
    Sherlock Holmes & the Voice of Terror (1942) U

Hound of the Baskervilles, The (novel)
    Hound of the Baskervilles, The (1939) TCF

Lost World, The (novel)
    Lost World, The (1925) FN
    Lost World, The (1960) TCF

Sherlock Holmes (from play by William Gillette)
    Sherlock Holmes (1916) ES
    Sherlock Holmes (1922) G
    Sherlock Holmes (1932) F

Silver Blaze (story)
    Murder at the Baskervilles (1941) ASTOR

Six Napoleons, The (short story)
    Pearl of Death, The (1944) U

Study in Scarlet, A (novel)
    Study in Scarlet, A (1933) F

Tragedy of the Koroska (story)
    Desert Sheik (1924) TRUART

DREISER, THEODORE

American Tragedy, An (novel)
    American Tragedy, An (1931) PAR
    Place in the Sun, A (1951) PAR

Jennie Gerhardt (novel)
    Jennie Gerhardt (1933) PAR

60

My Brother Paul (story)
    My Gal Sal (1942) TCF

Sister Carrie (novel)
    Carrie (1952) PAR

DRURY, ALLEN

Advise and Consent (novel)
    Advise and Consent (1962) COL

DU MAURIER, DAPHNE

Frenchman's Creek (novel)
    Frenchman's Creek (1944) PAR

My Cousin Rachel (novel)
    My Cousin Rachel (1952) TCF

Rebecca (novel)
    Rebecca (1940) UA

DU MAURIER, GEORGE

Dancers, The (play in collab. Viola Trees)
    Dancers, The (1925) F
    Dancers, The (1930) FN

Peter Ibbetson (novel, play by Raphael)
    Forever (1921) PAR
    Peter Ibbetson (1935) PAR

Trilby (novel)
    Trilby (1913) EQW
    Trilby (1923) FN
    Svengali (1931) WB

DUMAS, ALEXANDER

Camille (novel)
    Camille (1917) F
    Camille (1927) FN
    Camille (1937) MGM

Companions of Jehu, The (novel)
    Fighting Guardsman, The ((1945) COL

Corsican Brothers, The (novel)
    Corsican Brothers, The (1942) UA

Count of Monte Cristo, The (novel)
    Count of Monte Cristo, The (1913) PAR
    Monte Cristo (1922) F
    Count of Monte Cristo, The (1934) UA

Edmund Kean (novel)
    Stage Romance, A (1922) F

Man in the Iron Mask, The (novel)
    Iron Mask, The (1929) UA
    Man in the Iron Mask, The (1939) UA

Memoirs of a Physician (novel)
    Black Magic (1949) UA

Three Musketeers, The (novel)
    Three Musketeers, The (1921) UA
    Three Musketeers, The (1935) RKO
    Three Musketeers, The (1939) TCF
    Three Musketeers, The (1948) MGM

Twenty Years After (novel)
    At Sword's Point (1952) RKO

DUNNE, JOHN GREGORY

True Confessions (novel)
    True Confessions (1981) UA

E

EBERHART, MIGNON G.

From This Dark Stairway (novel)
    Murder of Dr. Harrigan, The (1936) FN

Mystery of Huntings End (story)
    Mystery House (1938) WB

While the Patient Slept (novel)
    While the Patient Slept (1935) FN

White Cockatoo, The (novel)
    White Cockatoo, The (1935) WB

EDENS, OLIVE

Heart and Hand (story)
    House Divided, A (1932) U

EDINGTON, MAY

Heart Is Young, The (story)
    False Madonna (1932) PAR

Purple and Fine Linen (story)
    Three Hours (1927) FN
    Adventure in Manhattan (1936) COL

Surprise Party (story)
      Studio Murder Mystery, The (1929) PAR

World Without End (novel)
      His Supreme Moment (1925) FN

EDMONDS, WALTER D.

Drums Along the Mohawk (novel)
      Drums Along the Mohawk (1939) TCF

Red Wheels Rolling (story)
      Chad Hanna (1940) TCF

Rome Haul (novel)
      Farmer Takes a Wife, The (1935) F
      Farmer Takes a Wife, The (1953) TCF

EGGLESTON, EDWARD

Hoosier Schoolmaster, The (novel)
      Hoosier Schoolmaster, The (1924) PDC
      Hoosier Schoolmaster, The (1935) MON

ELIOT, GEORGE

Romola (novel)
      Romola (1924) MG

ELLISON, HARLAN

Boy and His Dog, A (novel)
      Boy and His Dog, A (1975) LGJAF

ERSKINE, JOHN

Diane de Poitiers (story)
      Diane (1956) MGM

President's Mystery, The (story in collab. with
others)
      President's Mystery, The (1936) REP

Private Life of Helen of Troy, The (novel)
    Private Life of Helen of Troy, The (1927) FN

Sincerity (story)
    Lady Surrenders, A (1930) U

ERSKINE, LAURIE YORK

Renfrew Rides Again (novel)
    Fighting Mad (1939) MON

Renfrew Rides North (novel)
    Yukon Flight (1940) MON

Renfrew Rides the Range (novel)
    Crashing Thru (1939) MON

Renfrew's Long Trail (novel)
    Danger Ahead (1940) MON

ESMOND, H.V.

Under the Greenwood Tree (novel)
    Under the Greenwood Tree (1918) ART

F

FARAGO, ALEXANDER

Top Hat (play)
    Top Hat (1935) RKO

FARRELL, JAMES T.

Studs Lonigan (novel)
    Studs Lonigan (1960) UA

FAST, HOWARD

Fallen Angels (novel)
    Mirage (1965) U
    Jigsaw (1968) U

Spartacus (novel)
    Spartacus (1960) UI

Winston Affair, The (novel)
    Man in the Middle (1964) TCF

FAULKNER, WILLIAM

Hamlet, The (novel)
    Long Hot Summer, The (1958) TCF

Intruder in the Dust (novel)
      Intruder in the Dust (1949) MGM

Pylon (novel)
      Tarnished Angels, The (1958)

Reivers, The (novel)
      Reivers, The (1969) NG

Requiem for a Nun (novel)
      Sanctuary (1961) TCF

Sanctuary (novel)
      Story of Temple Drake, The (1933) PAR
      Sanctuary (1961) TCF

Sound and the Fury, The (novel)
      Sound and the Fury, The (1959) TCF

Tomorrow (short story)
      Tomorrow (1972) FILMGROUP

FERBER, EDNA

Cimarron (novel)
      Cimarron (1931) RKO
      Cimarron (1961) MGM

Classified (short story)
      Classified (1925) FN
      Hard to Get (1929) FN
      Hard to Get (1938) WB

Come and Get It (novel)
      Come and Get It (1936) UA

Dinner at Eight (play in collab. G.S. Kaufman)
      Dinner at Eight (1933) MGM

Fanny Herself (novel)
      No Woman Knows (1921) U

Giant (novel)
      Giant (1956) WB

Gigolo (short story)
      Gigolo (1926) PDC

Ice Palace (novel)
    Ice Palace (1960) WB

Mother Knows Best (short story)
    Mother Knows Best (1928) F

Old Man Minick (novel; play in collab. G.S. Kaufman)
    Minick (1925) WB
    Expert, The (1932) WB

Our Mrs. McChesney (short stories)
    Our Mrs. McChesney (1918) M

Royal Family, The (play in collab. G.S. Kaufman)
    Royal Family of Broadway, The (1930) PAR

Saratoga Trunk (novel)
    Saratoga Trunk (1945) WB

Show Boat (novel)
    Show Boat (1929) U
    Show Boat (1936) U
    Show Boat (1951) MGM

So Big (novel)
    So Big (1924) FN
    So Big (1932) WB
    So Big (1953) PAR

Stage Door (play in collab. G.S. Kaufman)
    Stage Door (1937) RKO

FINNEY, JACK

Assault on a Queen (novel)
    Assault on a Queen (1966) PAR

Five Against the House (story)
    Five Against the House (1955) COL

Good Neighbor Sam (novel)
    Good Neighbor Sam (1964) COL

House of Numbers (novel)
    House of Numbers (1957) MGM

Invasion of the Body Snatchers (novel)
    Invasion of the Body Snatchers (1956) AA
    Invasion of the Body Snatchers (1978) UA

FISHER, VARDIS

Mountain Men (novel)
    Jeremiah Johnson (1972) WB

FITCH, CLYDE

Bachelor, The (play)
    Virtuous Vamp, A (1919) FN

Barbara Frietchie (play from Whittier's poem)
    Barbara Frietchie (1915) M
    Barbara Frietchie (1924) PDC

Beau Brummel (play)
    Beau Brummel (1924) WB
    Beau Brummel (1954) MGM

Climbers, The (play)
    Climbers, The (1927) WB

Her Confessions (play)
    Wiser Sex, The (1932) PAR

Woman in the Case (play)
    Woman in the Case (1916) PAR

FITZGERALD, F. SCOTT

Babylon Revisited (short story)
    Last Time I Saw Paris, The (1954) MGM

Beautiful and the Damned, The (novel)
    Beautiful and the Damned, The (1922) WB

Great Gatsby, The (novel)
    Great Gatsby, The (1926) PAR
    Great Gatsby, The (1949) PAR
    Great Gatsby, The (1974) PAR

69

Head and Shoulders (short story)
    Chorus Girl's Romance (1920) M

Last Tycoon, The (novel)
    Last Tycoon, The (1976) PAR

Tender Is the Night (novel)
    Tender Is the Night (1962) TCF

FLAUBERT, GUSTAV

Madame Bovary (novel)
    Unholy Love (1932) HOD
    Madame Bovary (1949) MGM

FLAVIN, MARTIN

Broken Dishes (play)
    Too Young to Marry (1931) FN
    Love Begins at Twenty (1936) FN

Criminal Code, The (play)
    Criminal Code, The (1931) COL

Cross Roads (play)
    Age of Consent, The (1932) RKO

One Way Out (play)
    Convicted (1950) COL

FODOR, LADISLAUS

Charlie Chan in City in Darkness (play in collab.
G. Kaus)
    Charlie Chan in City in Darkness (1939) TCF

Church Mouse, The (play in collab. Paul Frank)
    Beauty and the Boss (1932) WB

Matura (play)
    Girls' Dormitory (1936) TCF

Night Before the Divorce, The (play in collab. G.
Kaus)
    Night Before the Divorce, The (1942) TCF

Suspicion (play)
    Wives Under Suspicion (1938) U

Unguarded Hour, The (play)
    Unguarded Hour, The (1936) MGM

White Lady (story in collab. G. Kaus)
    Isle of Missing Men (1942) MON

Woman Lies, A (play)
    Thunder in the Night (1935) F

FODOR, LAZLO

Birthday Gift (story)
    North to Alaska (1960) TCF

Footsteps in the Dark (play)
    Footsteps in the Dark (1941) WB

Jewel Robbery (play)
    Jewel Robbery (1932) WB

Kiss Before the Mirror, The (play)
    Kiss Before the Mirror, The (1933) RKO

FORBES, KATHRYN

Mama's Bank Account (novel)
    I Remember Mama (1948) RKO

FORESTER, C.S.

African Queen, The (novel)
    African Queen, The (1952) UA

Captain Horatio Hornblower (novel)
    Captain Horatio Hornblower (1951) WB

Commandos Strike at Dawn (story)
    Commandos Strike at Dawn (1942) COL

Eagle Squadron (story)
    Eagle Squadron (1942) U

71

Gun, The (novel)
    Pride and the Passion, The (1957) UA

FOWLER, GENE

Beau James (biography)
    Beau James (1957) PAR

Great Magoo, The (play in collab. B. Hecht)
    Shoot the Works (1934) PAR

FOX, JOHN

Heart of the Hills (novel)
    Heart of the Hills (1919) FN

Little Shepherd of Kingdom Come, The (novel)
    Kentucky Courage (1928) FBO
    Little Shepherd of Kingdom Come, The (1961) F

Trail of the Lonesome Pine (novel)
    Trail of the Lonesome Pine (1916) PAR
    Trail of the Lonesome Pine (1923) PAR
    Trail of the Lonesome Pine (1936) PAR

Valley of the Wolf (story)
    Hill Billy, The (1924) APA

FRANCE, ANATOLE

Crime of Sylvestre Bonnard (novel)
    Chasing Yesterday (1935) RKO

Red Lily, The (novel)
    Red Lily, The (1924) MG

FRANK, LEONARD

Karl and Anna (novel)
    Homecoming (1928) PAR
    Desire Me (1947) MGM

72

FRANKAU, GILBERT

Christopher Strong (novel)
    Christopher Strong (1933) RKO

If I Marry Again (novel)
    If I Marry Again (1925) FN

FRANKEN, ROSE

Another Language (play)
    Another Language (1933) MGM

Claudia (play)
    Claudia (1943) TCF

Claudia and David (stories)
    Claudia and David (1946) TCF

FRANKLIN, EDGAR

Adopted Father, The (novel)
    Twenty Dollars a Week (1924) AJ
    Working Man, The (1933) WB
    Everybody's Old Man (1936) TCF

FREEMAN, DEVERY

Taps (novel)
    Taps (1981) TCF

FRINGS, KETTI

Mr. Sycamore (play)
    Mr. Sycamore (1975) FV

FUCHS, DANIEL

Crazy Over Pigeons (short story)
    Day the Bookies Wept, The (1939) RKO

Low Company (novel)
    Gangster, The (1947) AA

73

G

GALE, ZONA

Miss Lulu Bett (novel, play)
    What Every Woman Knows (1921) PAR

Way, The (novel)
    When Strangers Meet (1934) LIB

GALLICO, PAUL

Adventures of Joe Smith, American (story)
    Big Operator, The (1959) MGM

Matilda (novel)
    Matilda (1978) AI

No Time to Marry (short story)
    No Time to Marry (1938) COL

Poseiden Adventure, The (novel)
    Poseiden Adventure, The (1972) TCF

Romance of Henry Menafee, The (short story)
    Merry Andrew (1958) MGM

Thomasina (novel)
    Three Lives of Thomasina, The (1963) BV

Trial by Terror (story)
    Assignment - Paris (1952) COL

Wedding Present (short story)
    Wedding Present (1936) PAR

GALSWORTHY, JOHN

Escape (play)
    Escape (1948) TCF

First and the Last, The (story)
    Stranger, The (1924) PAR

Forsyte Saga, The (novels)
    That Forsyte Woman (1949) MGM

One More River (story)
    One More River (1934) U

White Monkey, The (novel)
    White Monkey, The (1925) FN

GANN, ERNEST K.

Blaze of Noon (novel)
    Blaze of Noon (1947) PAR

Fate Is the Hunter (novel)
    Fate Is the Hunter (1964) TCF

Fiddler's Green (novel)
    Raging Tide, The (1951) U

High and the Mighty, The (novel)
    High and the Mighty, The (1954) WB

Island in the Sky (novel)
    Island in the Sky (1953) WB

Soldier of Fortune (novel)
    Soldier of Fortune (1955) TCF

Twilight for the Gods (novel)
    Twilight for the Gods (1958) UI

75

GARDNER, EARL STANLEY

Case of the Caretaker's Cat, The (novel)
    Case of the Black Cat (1936) FN

Case of the Curious Bride, The (novel)
    Case of the Curious Bride, The (1935) FN

Case of the Howling Dog, The (novel)
    Case of the Howling Dog, The (1934) WB

Case of the Lucky Legs, The (novel)
    Case of the Lucky Legs, The (1935) FN

Case of the Velvet Claws, The (novel)
    Case of the Velvet Claws, The (1936) WB

Fugitive Gold (novel)
    Special Investigator (1936) RKO

GARDNER, HERB

Thieves (play)
    Thieves (1977) PAR

GARDNER, JOHN

Complete State of Death, A (novel)
    Stone Killer, The (1973) COL

GARDNER, LEONARD

Fat City (novel)
    Fat City (1972) COL

GARFIELD, BRIAN

Death Wish (novel)
    Death Wish (1974) PAR

GARLAND, HAMLIN

Cavanaugh, Forest Ranger (novel)
    Ranger of the Big Pines, The (1925) VIT

GARY, ROMAIN

Colors of the Day, The (novel)
    Man Who Understood Women, The (1959) TCF

Lady L (novel)
    Lady L (1966) MGM

GATES, ELEANOR

Poor Little Rich Girl, The (play)
    Poor Little Rich Girl, The (1917) ART

GENET, JEAN

Balcony, The (play)
    Balcony, The (1963) COF

Deathwatch (play)
    Deathwatch (1967) ATR

GEORGE, PETER

Red Alert (novel)
    Dr. Strangelove (1964) COL

GERARD, JAMES W.

My Four Years in Germany (nonfiction)
    My Four Years in Germany (1918) SR

GEROULD, KATHERINE FULLERTON

Conquistador (novel)
    Yankee Senor (1926) F
    Romance of the Rio Grande (1929) F
    Romance of the Rio Grande (1940) TCF

GIBSON, WILLIAM

Cobweb, The (novel)
    Cobweb, The (1955) MGM

Miracle Worker, The (play)
    Miracle Worker, The (1962) UA

Two for the Seesaw (play)
    Two for the Seesaw (1962) UA

GILBRETH, FRANK B.

Belles on Their Toes (novel in collab. Ernestine Carew)
    Belles on Their Toes (1952) TCF

Cheaper by the Dozen (novel)
    Cheaper by the Dozen (1950) TCF

GILL, DEREK

Dove (nonfiction in collab. R.L. Graham)
    Dove, The (1974) PAR

GILLETTE, WILLIAM

Secret Service (play)
    Secret Service (1916) ES
    Secret Service (1919) PAR
    Secret Service (1931) RKO

Sherlock Holmes (play based on A.C. Doyle's stories)
    Sherlock Holmes (1922) G
    Sherlock Holmes (1932) F
    Adventures of Sherlock Holmes, The (1939) TCF

GIRAUDOUX, JEAN

Madwoman of Chaillot, The (play)
    Madwoman of Chaillot, The (1969) WB/SA

GLASGOW, ELLEN

In This Our Life (novel)
    In This Our Life (1942) WB

GLEASON, JAMES

Is Zat So? (play)
    Is Zat So? (1927) FN
    Two Fisted (1935) PAR

Shannons of Broadway, The (play)
    Goodbye Broadway (1938) U

GLYN, ELINOR

Beyond the Rocks (short story)
    Beyond the Rocks (1922) PAR

Career of Catherine Bush, The (novel)
    Career of Catherine Bush, The (1919) PAR

His Hour (short story)
    His Hour (1924) MG

It (short story)
    It (1927) PAR

Man and His Moment, The (novel)
    Mad Hour, The (1920) FN

Reason Why, The (novel)
    Soul Mates (1926) MGM

Three Weeks (novel)
    Three Weeks (1924) MG

Vicissitudes of Evangeline (story)
    Red Hair (1928) PAR

GODDEN, RUMER

Battle of the Villa Fiorita, The (novel)
    Battle of the Villa Fiorita, The (1965) WB

GOGOL, NIKOLAI

Taras Bulba (novel)
    Taras Bulba (1962) UA

GOLDEN, JOHN

After Tomorrow (play in collab. Hugh Strange)
    After Tomorrow (1932) F

Salt Water (play in collab. with others)
    Salt Water (1933) U

Three Wise Fools (play)
    Three Wise Fools (1923) G

GOLDMAN, JAMES

They Might Be Giants (play)
    They Might Be Giants (1971) U

GOLDMAN, WILLIAM

Magic (novel)
    Magic (1978) TCF

Marathon Man (novel)
    Marathon Man (1976) PAR

GOLDSMITH, OLIVER

Vicar of Wakefield, The (novel)
    Vicar of Wakefield, The (1916) PAT

GOODHART, WILLIAM

Generation (play)
    Generation (1969) AVCO

GOODRICH, FRANCES

Anne Frank: The Diary of a Young Girl (play in collab. A. Hackett)
    Diary of Anne Frank, The (1959) TCF

Up Pops the Devil (play in collab. A. Hackett)
    Thanks for the Memory (1938) PAR

GOODWIN, JOHN

Avenger, The (novel)
    Avenger, The (1933) MON

GORDON, LEON

Garden of Weeds, The (play in collab. Doris Marquetta)
    Garden of Weeds, The (1924) PAR

White Cargo (play)
    White Cargo (1942) MGM

GORDON, RUTH

Over 21 (play)
    Over 21 (1945) COL

Very Rich Woman, A (story)
    Rosie! (1967) U

Years Ago (play)
    Actress, The (1953) MGM

GRACZYK, ED

Come Back to the Five & Dime, Jimmy Dean, Jimmy Dean (play)
    Come Back to the Five & Dime, Jimmy Dean, Jimmy Dean (1982) C

GRADY, JAMES

Three Days of the Condor (novel)
    Three Days of the Condor (1975) PAR

GRAHAM, ROBIN LEE

Dove (nonfiction in collab. D. Gill)
    Dove, The (1974) PAR

GRAHAME, KENNETH

Wind in the Willows, The (novel)
    Adventures of Ichabod and Mr. Toad, The (anim.
    1949) RKO

GRANT, JAMES EDWARD

Green Shadow, The (novel)
    Muss 'Em Up (19356) RKO

Lady Comes to Burkburnett, A (story)
    Boom Town (1940) MGM

Trouble in B Flat (story)
    I Can't Give You Anythng but Love, Baby (1940)
    U

GRANT, MAXWELL

Fox Hound, The (story)
    International Crime (1938) GN

Shadow, The (stories)
    Shadow Strikes, The (1937) GN

GREEN, PAUL

House of Connelly, The (play)
    Carolina (1934) F

GREENE, GRAHAM

Comedians, The (novel)
    Comedians, The (1967) MGM

End of the Affair, The (novel)
    End of the Affair, The (1955) COL

Honorary Consul, The (novel)
    Beyond the Limit (1983) PAR

Labyrinthine Ways, The (novel)
    Fugitive, The (1947) RKO

Ministry of Fear (novel)
    Ministry of Fear (1945) PAR

Orient Express (novel)
    Orient Express (1934) F

Quiet American, The (novel)
    Quiet American, The (1958) UA

This Gun for Hire (novel)
    This Gun for Hire (1942) PAR
    Short Cut to Hell (1957) PAR

GREENE, WARD

Death in the Deep South (novel)
    They Won't Forget (1937) WB

GREY, ZANE

Bee Hunter (short story)
    Under the Tonto Rim (1933) PAR

Border Legion, The (novel)
    Border Legion, The (1918) THH
    Border Legion, The (1930) PAR
    Last Round-Up, The (1934) PAR
    Border Legion, The (1940) REP

Born to the West (story)
    Born to the West (1926) PAR
    Born to the West (1936) PAR

Call of the Canyon, The (novel)
    Call of the Canyon, The (1923) PAR

Canyon Walls (story)

Smoke Lightning (1933) F

Code of the West (novel)
    Code of the West (1925) PAR
    Home on the Range (1935) PAR

Desert Gold (novel)
    Desert Gold (1926) PAR
    Desert Gold (1936) PAR

Desert of Wheat, The (novel)
    Riders of the Dawn (1920) HOD

Fighting Caravans (novel)
    Fighting Caravans (1931) PAR
    Wagon Wheels (1934) PAR

Golden Dreams (story)
    Rocky Mountain Mystery (1935) PAR

Heritage of the Desert, The (novel)
    Heritage of the Desert, The (1924) PAR
    Heritage of the Desert, The (1933) PAR
    Heritage of the Desert, The (1939) PAR

King of the Royal Mounted (cartoon strip)
    King of the Royal Mounted (1936) TCF
    Yukon Patrol, The (1942) REP

Last of the Duanes, The (novel)
    Last of the Duanes, The (1919) F
    Last of the Duanes, The (1924) F
    Last of the Duanes, The (1930) F
    Last of the Duanes, The (1941) F

Last Trail, The (story)
    Last Trail, The (1927) F
    Last Trail, The (1933) F

Light of the Western Stars, The (novel)
    Light of the Western Stars, The (1918) SHU
    Light of the Western Stars, The (1925) PAR
    Light of the Western Stars, The (1930) PAR
    Light of the Western Stars, The (1940) MAB

Rainbow Trail, The (novel)
    Rainbow Trail, The (1918) F
    Rainbow Trail, The (1925) F

Rainbow Trail, The (1932) F

Riders of the Purple Sage (novel)
        Riders of the Purple Sage (1918) F
        Riders of the Purple Sage (1925) F
        Riders of the Purple Sage (1931) F
        Riders of the Purple Sage (1941) F

Roles (story)
        Changing Husbands (1924) PAR

Stairs of Sand (story)
        Arizona Mahoney (1937) PAR

Thunder Trail (novel)
        Thunder Trail (1938) PAR

Thundering Herd, The (novel)
        Thundering Herd, The (1925) PAR
        Thundering Herd, The (1934) PAR

To the Last Man (novel)
        To the Last Man (1923) PAR
        To the Last Man (1933) PAR

To the Law (story)
        Thunder Mountain (1947) RKO

Twin Sombreros (novel)
        Gunfighters (1947) COL

Vanishing American, The (novel)
        Vanishing American, The (1925) PAR
        Vanishing American, The (1955) REP

Wanderer of the Wasteland, The (novel)
        Wanderer of the Wasteland, The (1924) PAR
        Wanderer of the Wasteland, The (1935) PAR
        Wanderer of the Wasteland, The (1945) RKO

Water Hole, The (story)
        Water Hole, The (1928) PAR

West of the Pecos (novel)
        West of the Pecos (1934) RKO

Western Union (novel)
        Western Union (1941) TCF

Wild Horse Mesa (story)
    Wild Horse Mesa (1925) PAR
    Wild Horse Mesa (1933) PAR

Wildfire (novel)
    When Romance Rides (1922) G
    Red Canyon (1949) UI

GRIMM BROTHERS

Snow White (short story)
    Snow White (1916) EDU
    Snow White (1917) PAR
    Snow White and the Seven Dwarfs (1937) RKO
    Snow White and the Three Stooges (1961) TCF

Tom Thumb (short story)
    Tom Thumb (1958) MGM

GRUBB, DAVIS

Fools' Parade (novel)
    Fools' Parade (1971) COL

GUEST, JUDITH

Ordinary People (novel)
    Ordinary People (1980) PAR

GUITRY, SACHA

Bonne Chance (play)
    Lucky Partners (1940) RKO

Deburau (play)
    Lover of Camille, The (1924) WB

GUTHRIE, JR., A.B.

Big Sky, The (novel)
    Big Sky, The (1952) RKO

86

These Thousand Hills (novel)
    These Thousand Hills (1959) TCF

Way West, The (novel)
    Way West, The (1967) UA

GUTHRIE, WOODY

Bound for Glory (biography)
    Bound for Glory (1976) UA

HACKETT, ALBERT

Anne Frank: The Diary of a Young Girl (play in collab. F. Goodrich)
    Diary of Anne Frank, The (1959) TCF

Up Pops the Devil (play in collab. F. Goodrich)
    Thanks for the Memory (1938) PAR

HACKETT, WALTER

Afterwards (story)
    Their Big Moment (1934) RKO

Captain Applejack (play)
    Strangers of the Night (1923) M

Espionage (play)
    Espionage (1937) MGM

Love Under Fire (play)
    Love Under Fire (1937) TCF

Other Men's Wives (play)
    Sweethearts and Wives (1930) FN

HAGAN, JAMES

One Sunday Afternoon (play)
        One Sunday Afternoon (1933) PAR
        Strawberry Blonde, The (1941) WB
        One Sunday Afternoon (1948) WB

HAGGARD, H. RIDER

King Solomon's Mines (novel)
        King Solomon's Mines (1950) MGM

Moon of Israel, The (novel)
        Moon of Israel, The (1927) FBO

Return to King Solomon's Mines (novel)
        Watusi (1959) MGM

She (novel)
        She (1935) RKO

HAILEY, ARTHUR

Airport (novel)
        Airport (1970) U
        Airport '75 (1974) U
        Concorde: Airport '79, The (1979) U

Final Diagnosis, The (novel)
        Young Doctors, The (1961) UA

Hotel (novel)
        Hotel (1967) WB

HAINES, WILLIAM WISTER

Command Decision (play)
        Command Decision (1949) MGM

Slim (novel)
        Slim (1937) WB

HALE, EDWARD EVERETT

Man Without a Country, The (novel)
        Man Without a Country, The (1917) U

Man Without a Country, The (1925) WB

HALL, JAMES NORMAN

Botany Bay (novel in collab. C. Nordhoff)
    Botany Bay (1953) PAR

High Barbaree (novel in collab. C. Nordhoff)
    High Barbaree (1947) MGM

Hurricane, The (novel in collab. C. Nordhoff)
    Hurricane, The (1937) UA
    Hurricane, The (1979) PAR

Mutiny on the Bounty (novel in collab. C. Nordhoff)
    Mutiny on the Bounty (1935) MGM
    Mutiny on the Bounty (1962) MGM

No More Gas (novel in collab. C. Nordhoff)
    Tuttles of Tahiti, The (1942) RKO

HAMILTON, CLAYTON

Girl Habit, The (play in collab. A.E. Thomas)
    Girl Habit, The (1931) PAR

Thirty Days (play in collab. A.E. Thomas)
    Thirty Days (1922) PAR

HAMILTON, DONALD

Ambushers, The (novel)
    Ambushers, The (1967) COL

Big Country, The (novel)
    Big Country, The (1958) UA

Death of a Citizen (novel)
    Silencers, The (1966) COL

Murderers' Row (novel)
    Murderers' Row (1966) COL

Violent Men, The (novel)
    Violent Men, The (1955) COL

Wrecking Crew, The (novel)
    Wrecking Crew, The (1969) COL

HAMMERSTEIN II, OSCAR

New Moon (operetta)
    New Moon (1930) MGM
    New Moon (1940) MGM

New Toys (play in collab. MIlton H. Gropper)
    New Toys (1925) FN

HAMMETT, DASHIELL

Glass Key, The (novel)
    Glass Key, The (1935) PAR
    Glass Key, The (1942) PAR

Maltese Falcon, The (novel)
    Maltese Falcon, The (1931) WB
    Satan Met a Lady (1936) WB
    Maltese Falcon, The (1941) WB

On the Make (story)
    Mr. Dynamite (1935) U

Red Harvest (novel)
    Roadhouse Nights (1930) PAR

Thin Man, The (novel)
    Thin Man, The (1934) MGM

HANSBERRY, LORRAINE

Raisin in the Sun, A (play)
    Raisin in the Sun, A (1961) COL

HARDY, THOMAS

Tess of the D'Urbervilles (novel)
    Tess of the D'Urbervilles (1924) PAR

HARGROVE, MARION

Girl He Left Behind, The (novel)
    Girl He Left Behind, The (1956) WB

See Here, Private Hargrove (novel)
    See Here, Private Hargrove (1944) MGM

HARRIS, ELMER

Brothers (story)
    Forbidden Woman, The (1927) PAT

Johnny Belinda (play)
    Johnny Belinda (1948) WB

Sham (play in collab. Ethel Clayton)
    Sham (1921) PAR

HARRIS, FRANK

Reminiscences of a Cowboy (novel)
    Cowboy (1958) COL

HARRIS, MARK

Bang the Drum Slowly (novel)
    Bang the Drum Slowly (1973) PAR

HART, MOSS

Act One (autobiography)
    Act One (1963) WB

Decision of Christopher Blake, The (play)
    Decision of Christopher Blake, The (1948) WB

George Washington Slept Here (play)
    George Washington Slept Here (1942) WB

Lady in the Dark (play)
    Lady in the Dark (1944) PAR

Man Who Came to Dinner, The (play in collab. G.S.
Kaufman)
    Man Who Came to Dinner, The (1942) WB

Once in a Lifetime (play in collab. G.S. Kaufman)
    Once in a Lifetime (1932) U

Winged Victory (play)
    Winged Victory (1944) TCF

You Can't Take It With You (play in collab. G.S.
Kaufman)
    You Can't Take It With You (1938) COL

HARTE, BRET

Half Breed, The (short story)
    Half Breed, The (1916) FAT
    Half Breed, The (1922) FN

Idyl of Red Gulch (short story)
    Man From Red Gulch (1925) PDC

Jordan Is a Hard Road (short story)
    Jordan Is a Hard Road (1915) TRI

M'Liss (novel)
    M'Liss (1918) ART
    M'Liss (1936) RKO

Outcasts of Poker Flat, The (short story)
    Outcasts of Poker Flat, The (1937) RKO
    Outcasts of Poker Flat, The (1952) TCF

Saint of Calamity Gulch (short story)
    Taking a Chance (1929) F

Salomy Jane's Kiss (story in collab. P. Armstrong)
    Wild Girl (1932) F

Tennessee's Partner (short story)
    Flaming Forties (1925) PDC
    Golden Princess, The (1925) PAR
    Tennessee's Partner (1955) RKO

HATCH, ERIC

1101 Park Avenue (short story)
    My Man Godfrey (1936) U
    My Man Godfrey (1957) U

Road Show (novel)
    Road Show (1941) UA

Unexpected Uncle (novel)
    Unexpected Uncle (1941) RKO

Year of the Horse, The (short story)
    Horse in the Gray Flannel Suit, The (1968) BV

HAWTHORNE, NATHANIEL

Dr. Heidegger's Experiment (short story)
    Twice Told Tales (1964) UA

House of the Seven Gables, The (novel)
    House of the Seven Gables, The (1940) U
    Twice Told Tales (1964) UA

Rappaccini's Daughter (short story)
    Twice Told Tales (1964) UA

Scarlet Letter, The (novel)
    Scarlet Letter, The (1917) F
    Scarlet Letter, The (1926) MGM

HAYCOX, ERNEST

Bugles in the Afternoon (novel)
    Bugles in the Afternoon (1952) WB

Canyon Passage (story)
    Canyon Passage (1946) U

Stage to Lordsburg (short story)
    Stagecoach (1939) UA
    Stagecoach (1966) TCF

Trail Town (novel)
    Abilene Town (1946) UA

HECHT, BEN

Florentine Dagger, The (novel)

Florentine Dagger, The (1935) WB

Front Page, The (play in collab. C. MacArthur)
    Front Page, The (1931) UA
    His Girl Friday (1940) COL
    Front Page, The (1974) U

Gaily, Gaily (novel)
    Gaily, Gaily (1969) UA

Great Magoo, The (play in collab. G. Fowler)
    Shoot the Works (1934) PAR

Hazel Flagg (play)
    Living It Up (1954) PAR

Jumbo (play in collab. C. MacArthur)
    Jumbo (1962) MGM

Ladies and Gentlemen (play in collab. C. MacArthur)
    Perfect Strangers (1950) WB

Miracle in the Rain (novel)
    Miracle in the Rain (1956) WB

Twentieth Century (play in collab. C. MacArthur)
    Twentieth Century (1934) COL
    Streamline Express (1935) MAS

HEINLEIN, ROBERT A.

Destination Moon (novel)
    Destination Moon (1950) EL

HELLER, JOSEPH

Catch-22 (novel)
    Catch-22 (1970) PAR

HELLMAN, LILLIAN

Another Part of the Forest (play)
    Another Part of the Forest (1948) UI

Children's Hour, The (play)

These Three (1936) UA
    Children's Hour, The (1962) UA

Little Foxes, The (play)
    Little Foxes, The (1941) RKO

Pentimento (novel)
    Julia (1977) TCF

Searching Wind, The (play)
    Searching Wind, The (1946) PAR

Toys in the Attic (play)
    Toys in the Attic (1963) UA

Watch on the Rhine (play)
    Watch on the Rhine (1943) WB

HEMINGWAY, ERNEST

Farewell to Arms, A (novel)
    Farewell to Arms, A (1932) PAR
    Farewell to Arms, A (1958) TCF

For Whom the Bell Tolls (novel)
    For Whom the Bell Tolls (1943) PAR

Islands in the Stream (novel)
    Islands in the Stream (1977) PAR

Killers, The (short story)
    Killers, The (1946) U
    Killers, The (1964) U

My Old Man (short story)
    Under My Skin (1950) TCF

Old Man and the Sea, The (novel)
    Old Man and the Sea, The (1958) WB

Short Happy Life of Francis Macomber, The (short story)
    Macomber Affair, The (1947) UA

Snows of Kilimanjaro, The (short story)
    Snows of Kilimanjaro, The (1952) TCF

Sun Also Rises, The (novel)
    Sun Also Rises, The (1957) TCF

To Have and Have Not (novel)
    To Have and Have Not (1944) WB
    Breaking Point, The (1950) WB

HENRY, O.

Arizona Kid, The (short story)
    Arizona Kid, The (1930) F

Badge of Policeman O'Roon, The (short story)
    Doctor Rhythm (1938) PAR

Caballero's Way, The (short story)
    In Old Arizona (1929) F
    Cisco Kid, The (1931) F
    Return of the Cisco Kid (1939) TCF

Clarion Call, The (short story)
    O. Henry's Full House (1952) TCF

Cop and the Anthem, The (short story)
    O. Henry's Full House (1952) TCF

Double-Dyed Deceiver, The (short story)
    Texan, The (1930) PAR
    Llano Kid, The (1939) PAR

Ghost of a Chance, The (short story)
    Ghost of a Chance (1919)

Gift of the Magi, The (short story)
    O. Henry's Full House (1952) TCF

Green Door, The (short story)
    Green Door, The (1917)

Last Leaf, The (short story)
    O. Henry's Full House (1952) TCF

Passing of Black Eagle, The (short story)
    Black Eagle (1948) COL

HENRY, WILL

Frontier Fury (novel)
    Pillars in the Sky (1956) U

McKenna's Gold (novel)
    McKenna's Gold (1969) COL

Who Rides With Wyatt (novel)
    Young Billy Young (1969) UA

HERBERT, F. HUGH

.Cornered (story)
    Road to Paradise (1930) FN

For Love or Money (story)
    This Happy Feeling (1958) U

Moon Is Blue, The (play)
    Moon Is Blue, The (1953) UA

HERBERT, JOHN

Fortune and Men's Eyes (play)
    Fortune and Men's Eyes (1971) MGM

HERGESHEIMER, JOSEPH

Bright Shawl, The (novel)
    Bright Shawl, The (1923) FN

Cytherea (novel)
    Cytherea (1924) FN

Java Head (novel)
    Java Head (1935) FD

Tampico (novel)
    Woman I Stole, The (1933) COL

Tol'able David (short story)
    Tol'able David (1921) FN
    Tol'able David (1930) COL

Wild Oranges (novel)

Wild Oranges (1924) MG

HERLIHY, JAMES LEO

All Fall Down (novel)
    All Fall Down (1962) MGM

Blue Denim (play in collab. William Noble)
    Blue Denim (1959) TCF

Midnight Cowboy (novel)
    Midnight Cowboy (1969) UA

HERSEY, JOHN

Bell for Adano, A (novel)
    Bell for Adano, A (1945) TCF

War Lover, The (novel)
    War Lover, The (1963) COL

HEYWARD, DUBOSE

Porgy (play in collab. Dorothy Heyward)
    Porgy and Bess (1959) COL

HICHENS, ROBERT

Bella Donna (novel)
    Temptation (1946) U

Garden of Allah, The (novel)
    Garden of Allah, The (1927) MGM
    Garden of Allah, The (1936) UA

Paradine Case, The (novel)
    Paradine Case, The (1948) SRO

Snake Bite (story)
    Lady Who Lied, The (1925) FN

Voice From the Minaret, The (play)
    Voice From the Minaret, The (1923) FN

HILTON, JAMES

Lost Horizon (novel)
    Lost Horizon (1937) COL
    Lost Horizon (1973) COL

Rage in Heaven (novel)
    Rage in Heaven (1941) MGM

Random Harvest (novel)
    Random Harvest (1942) MGM

So Well Remembered (novel)
    So Well Remembered (1947) RKO

We Are Not Alone (novel)
    We Are Not Alone (1939) WB

HINTON, S.E.

Outsiders, The (novel)
    Outsiders, The (1983) WB

Rumble Fish (novel)
    Rumble Fish (1983) U

Tex (novel)
    Tex (1982) BV

HOBART, ALICE TISDALE

Cup and the Sword, The (novel)
    This Earth Is Mine (1959) U

Oil for the Lamps of China (novel)
    Oil for the Lamps of China (1935) WB
    Law of the Tropics (1941) WB

HOBART, GEORGE V.

Experience (play)
    Experience (1921) PAR

Wildfire (play in collab. G. Broadhurst)

Wildfire (1925) VIT

HOBSON, LAURA Z.

Gentleman's Agreement (novel)
    Gentleman's Agreement (1947) TCF

HOFFE, MONCKTON

Lady Christilinda (play)
    Street Angel (1928) F

Lady Eve, The (short story)
    Lady Eve, The (1941) PAR
    Birds and the Bees, The (1956) PAR

Panthea (play)
    Panthea (1916) SEZ

Scent of Sweet Almonds (story)
    Pleasure Crazed (1929) F

HOMER

Iliad (story)
    Helen of Troy (1956) WB

Odyssey (story)
    Ulysses (1955) PAR

HOOVER, J. EDGAR

Persons in Hiding (nonfiction)
    Parole Fixer (1940) PAR
    Queen of the Mob (1940) PAR
    Undercover Doctor (1939) PAR

HOPE, ANTHONY

Captain Dieppe (novel)
    Adventure in Hearts (1919) PAR

Indiscretions of the Duchess (novel)

101

Naughty Duchess (1928) TIF

Prisoner of Zenda, The (novel; play version: Edward Rose)
      Prisoner of Zenda, The (1922) MGM
      Prisoner of Zenda, The (1937) UA
      Prisoner of Zenda, The (1952) MGM

Rupert of Hentzau (novel)
      Rupert of Hentzau (1923) SEZ

HOPWOOD, AVERY

Bat, The (play in collab. M.R. Rinehart)
      Bat, The (1926) UA
      Bat, The (1959) AA

Best People, The (play in collab. David Grey)
      Best People, The (1925) PAR
      Fast and Loose (1930) PAR

Getting Gertie's Garter (play in collab. W. Collison)
      Getting Gertie's Garter (1927) PDC
      Getting Gertie's Garter (1946) UA

Gold Diggers, The (play)
      Gold Diggers of Broadway, The (1929) WB
      Gold Diggers of 1933 (1933) WB
      Painting the Clouds With Sunshine (1951) WB

Little Miss Bluebeard (play)
      Her Wedding Night (1930) PAR

Naughty Cinderella (play)
      Good and Naughty (1926) PAR
      This Is the Night (1932) PAR

Nobody's Widow (play)
      Nobody's Widow (1927) PDC

Our Little Wife (play)
      Our Little Wife (1918) G

Pouche (short story in collab. with others)
      This Is the Night (1932) PAR

Tumble In (play in collab. M.R. Rinehart)
    Seven Days (1925) UDC

Why Men Leave Home (play)
    Why Men Leave Home (1924) FN

HORNBLOW, ARTHUR

By Right of Conquest (novel)
    Isle of Conquest, The (1919) SEZ

HORNUNG, E.W.

Raffles, the Amateur Cracksman (novel)
    Raffles, the Amateur Cracksman (1917) HWF
    Raffles (1925) U
    Raffles (1930) UA
    Raffles (1940) UA

HORWITZ, JULIUS

Natural Enemies (novel)
    Natural Enemies (1979) CINEMA 5

HOUSTON, JAMES

White Dawn, The (novel)
    White Dawn, The (1974) PAR

HOWARD, SIDNEY

Half Gods (play)
    Free Love (1930) U

Late Christopher Bean, The (play)
    Christopher Bean (1933) MGM

Lucky Sam McCarver (play)
    We're All Gamblers (1927) PAR

Ned McCobb's Daughter (play)
    Ned McCobb's Daughter (1928) PAT

Silver Cord, The (play)
     Silver Cord, The (1933) RKO

They Knew What They Wanted (play)
     Secret Hour, The (1928) PAR
     Lady to Love, A (1930) MGM
     They Knew What They Wanted (1940) RKO

Yellow Jack (play)
     Yellow Jack (1938) MGM

HUBBARD, ELBERT

Message to Garcia, A (essay)
     Message to Garcia, A (1936) TCF

HUDSON, W.H.

Green Mansions (novel)
     Green Mansions (1959) MGM

HUGHES, RUPERT

Bitterness (story)
     Look Your Best (1933) G

Canavan (story)
     It Had to Happen (1936) TCF

Excuse Me (play)
     Excuse Me (1925) MG

Kidnapped (story)
     Miss Fane's Baby Is Stolen (1934) PAR

No One Man (novel)
     No One Man (1932) PAR

Obscurity (story)
     Breach of Promise (1932) WW

Old Nest, The (short story)
     Old Nest, The (1921) G

Patent Leather Kid, The (story)

Patent Leather Kid, The (1927) FN

Pop (story)
    Remembrance (1922) G

Scratch My Back (story)
    Scratch My Back (1920) G

Unpardonable Sin, The (novel)
    Unpardonable Sin, The (1919) GAR

HUGHES, THOMAS

Tom Brown's School Days (novel)
    Tom Brown's School Days (1940) TCF

HUGO, VICTOR

Hunchback of Notre Dame, The (novel)
    Hunchback of Notre Dame, The (1923) U
    Hunchback of Notre Dame, The (1939) RKO

Les Miserables (novel)
    Les Miserables (1917) F
    Les Miserables (1927) U
    Les Miserables (1935) TC
    Les Miserables (1952) TCF
    Sea Devils (1953) RKO

Man Who Laughs, The (novel)
    Man Who Laughs, The (1928) U

HUIE, WILLIAM BRADFORD

Americanization of Emily, The (novel)
    Americanization of Emily, The (19564) MGM

Hero of Iwo Jima, The (story)
    Outsider, The (1962) U

Mud on the Stars (novel)
    Wild River (1960) TCF

Revolt of Mamie Stover, The (novel)
    Revolt of Mamie Stover, The (1956) TCF

105

HULL, EDITH M.

Desert Healer, The (novel)
    Old Loves and New (1926) FN

Sheik, The (novel)
    Sheik, The (1921) PAR

HULME, KATHRYN C.

Nun's Story, The (novel)
    Nun's Story, The (1959) WB

HUME, CYRIL

Wife of the Centaur, The (novel)
    Wife of the Centaur, The (1924) MG

HUNTER, EVAN

Blackboard Jungle, The (novel)
    Blackboard Jungle, The (1955) MG

Buddwing (novel)
    Mister Buddwing (1966) MGM

Every Little Crook and Nanny (novel)
    Every Little Crook and Nanny (1972) MGM

Last Summer (novel)
    Last Summer (1969) AA

Matter of Conviction, A (novel)
    Young Savages, The (1961) UA

Strangers When We Meet (novel)
    Strangers When We Meet (1960) COL

HURST, FANNY

Back Pay (novel)
    Back Pay (1922) PAR

Back Pay (1930) FN

Back Street (novel)
    Back Street (1932) U
    Back Street (1941) U
    Back Street (1961) UI

Give the Little Girl a Hand (story)
    Painted Angel (1930) FN

Humoresque (novel)
    Humoresque (1920) PAR
    Humoresque (1946) WB

Imitation of Life (novel)
    Imitation of Life (1934) U
    Imitation of Life (1959) UI

Lummox (play)
    Lummox (1930) UA

Mannequin (story)
    Mannequin (1926) PAR

Nth Commandment, The (short story)
    Nth Commandment, The (1923) PAR

Roulette (novel)
    Wheel of Chance (1928) FN

Sister Act (novel)
    Four Daughters (1938) WB
    Four Wives (1939) WB

Star Dust (short story)
    Star Dust (1922) FN

Untamed Lady, The (story)
    Untamed Lady, The (1926) PAR

HUXLEY, ALDOUS

Giaconda Smile, The (short story)
    Woman's Revenge, A (1948) UI

HYMER, JOHN D.

Alias the Deacon (play)
    Half a Sinner (1924) U
    Alias the Deacon (1927) U
    Alias the Deacon (1940) U

East Is West (play in collab. S. Shipman)
    East Is West (1930) U

Fast Life (play in collab. S. Shipman)
    Fast Life (1929) FN

Pay-Off, The (play in collab. S. Shipman)
    Pay-Off, The (1930) RKO

Scarlet Pages (play in collab. S. Shipman)
    Scarlet Pages (1930) FN

I

IBANEZ, VINCENTE B.

Blood and Sand (novel)
    Blood and Sand (1922) PAR
    Blood and Sand (1941) TCF

Four Horsemen of the Apocalypse, The (novel)
    Four Horsemen of the Apocalypse, The (1921) M
    Four Horsemen of the Apocalypse, The (1962)
    MGM

Mare Nostrum (novel)
    Mare Nostrum (1926) MGM

Temptress, The (novel)
    Temptress, The (1926) MGM

Torrent (novel)
    Ibanez's Torrent (1926) MGM

IBSEN, HENRIK

Doll's House, A (play)
    Doll's House, A (1918) ART
    Doll's House, A (1922) UA

Enemy of the People, An (play)
    Enemy of the People, An (1980) WB

INGE, WILLIAM

Bus Stop (play)
    Bus Stop (1956) TCF

Come Back, Little Sheba (play)
    Come Back, Little Sheba (1952) PAR

Dark at the Top of the Stairs, The (play)
    Dark at the Top of the Stairs, The (1960) WB

Good Luck, Miss Wyckoff (novel)
    Good Luck, Miss Wyckoff (1979) Bel Air

Loss of Roses, A (play)
    Stripper, The (1963) TCF

IONESCO, EUGENE

Rhinoceros (play)
    Rhinoceros (1974) AFT

IRVING, JOHN

World According to Garp, The (novel)
    World According To Garp, The (1982) WB

IRVING, WASHINGTON

Legend of Sleepy Hollow, The (short story)
    Headless Horseman, The (1922) HOD
    Adventures of Ichabod and Mr. Toad (anim.
    1949) RKO
    Legend of Sleepy Hollow, The (1979) SUNN

IRWIN, MARGARET

Young Bess (novel)
    Young Bess (1953) MGM

ISHERWOOD, CHRISTOPHER

I Am a Camera (stories)
    Cabaret (1972) AA

J

JACKSON, CHARLES R.

Lost Weekend, The (novel)
    Lost Weekend, The (1945) PAR

JACKSON, HELEN HUNT

Ramona (novel)
    Ramona (1910)
    Ramona (1916) CLUNE
    Ramona (1928) UA
    Ramona (1936) TCF

JACKSON, SHIRLEY

Bird's Nest, The (novel)
    Lizzie (1957) MGM

Haunting of Hill House, The (novel)
    Haunting, The (1963) MGM

JACOBS, W.W.

Interruption, The (short story)
    Footsteps in the Fog (1955) COL

Money Box, The (short story)
    Our Relations (1936) MGM

JAMES, HENRY

Aspern Papers, The (novel)
    Lost Moment, The (1947) UI

Daisy Miller (novel)
    Daisy Miller (1974) PAR

Washington Square (novel)
    Heiress, The (1949) PAR

JAMES, RIAN

Crooner (novel)
    Crooner (1932) FN

Hat Check Girl (novel)
    Hat Check Girl (1932) F

Love Is a Racket (novel)
    Love Is a Racket (1932) FN

Some Call It Love (story)
    Parachute Jumper (1933) WB

White Parade, The (novel)
    White Parade, The (1934) F

JAMES, WILL

Lone Cowboy, The (novel)
    Shoot Out (1971) U

Sand (novel)
    Sand (1949) TCF

Smoky (novel)
    Smoky (1934) F
    Smoky (1946) TCF

JESSUP, RICHARD

Cincinnati Kid, The (novel)
    Cincinnati Kid, The (1965) MGM

Cunning and the Haunted, The (story)
    Young Don't Cry, The (1957) COL

JOHNSON, OWEN

Children of Divorce (novel)
    Children of Divorce (1927) PAR

Lawrenceville School Stories (stories)
    Happy Years, The (1950) MGM

Salamander, The (novel)
    Enemy Sex, The (1924) PAR

Virtuous Wives (story)
    Virtuous Wives (1918) FN

Woman Gives In, The (novel)
    Woman Gives In, The (1920) FN

JOHNSTON, MARY

Audrey (novel)
    Audrey (1916) PAR

To Have and to Hold (novel)
    To Have and to Hold (1916) PAR
    To Have and to Hold (1922) PAR

JONES, JAMES

From Here to Eternity (novel)
    From Here to Eternity (1953) COL

Some Came Running (novel)
    Some Came Running (1959) MGM

JONES, LEROI

Slave (play)

Fable, A (1971) MFR

JONES, MERVYN

John and Mary (novel)
    John and Mary (1969) TCF

JOYCE, JAMES

Ulysses (novel)
    Ulysses (1967) CDI

K

KANIN, GARSON

Born Yesterday (play)
    Born Yesterday (1950) COL

Do Re Mi (short story)
    Girl Can't Help It, The (1956) TCF

Live Wire, The (play)
    Right Approach, The (1961) TCF

Rat Race, The (play)
    Rat Race, The (1960) PAR

KANTOR, MACKINLEY

Arouse and Beware (novel)
    Man From Dakota (1940) MGM

Gentle Annie (novel)
    Gentle Annie (1945) MGM

Glory for Me (novel)
    Best Years of Our Lives, The (1946) RKO

God, My Country (novel)
    Follow Me, Boys (1966) BV

Gun Crazy (short story)
    Gun Crazy (1950) UA

Happy Land (novel)
    Happy Land (1943) TCF

Romance of Rosy Ridge (story)
    Romance of Rosy Ridge (1947) MGM

Voice of Bugle Ann, The (novel)
    Voice of Bugle Ann, The (1936) MGM

KAUFMAN, BEL

Up the Down Staircase (novel)
    Up the Down Staircase (1967) WB

KAUFMAN, GEORGE S.

Beggar on Horseback (play in collab. Marc Connelly)
    Beggar on Horseback (1925) PAR

Butter and Egg Man, The (play)
    Butter and Egg Man, The (1928) FN
    Tenderfoot, The (1932) FN
    Dance Charlie Dance (1937) WB
    Angel From Texas, An (1940) WB

Dark Tower, The (play in collab. Alexander
Woollcott)
    Man With Two Faces, The (1934) FN

Dinner at Eight (play in collab. Edna Ferber)
    Dinner at Eight (1933) MGM

Dulcy (play in collab. Marc Connelly)
    Dulcy (1923) FN
    Not So Dumb (1930) MGM
    Dulcy (1940) MGM

First Lady (play in collab. Kathryn Dayton)
    First Lady (1937) WB

George Washington Slept Here (play in collab. Moss
Hart)
    George Washington Slept Here (1942) WB

June Moon (play in collab. Ring Lardner)
    June Moon (1931) PAR
    Blonde Trouble (1937) PAR

Late George Apley, The (play in collab. J.P.
Marquand)
    Late George Apley, The (1947) TCF

Man Who Came to Dinner, The (play in collab. Moss
Hart)
    Man Who Came to Dinner, The (1942) WB

Merton of the Movies (play in collab. Marc
Connelly)
    Merton of the Movies (1924) PAR
    Merton of the Movies (1947) MGM

Minick (play in collab. Edna Ferber)
    Welcome Home (1925) PAR
    Expert, The (1932) WB

Once in a Lifetime (play in collab. Moss Hart)
    Once in a Lifetime (1932) U

Royal Family, The (play in collab. Edna Ferber)
    Royal Family of Broadway, The (1930) PAR

Solid Gold Cadillac, The (play in collab. Howard
Teichman)
    Solid Gold Cadillac, The (1956) COL

Stage Door (play in collab. Edna Ferber)
    Stage Door (1937) RKO

Three Sailors and a Girl (play)
    Three Sailors and a Girl (1953) WB

To the Ladies (play in collab. Marc Connelly)
    To the Ladies (1923) PAR
    Elmer and Elsie (1934) PAR

You Can't Take It With You (play in collab. Moss
Hart)
    You Can't Take It With You (1938) COL

KAUS, GINA

118

Dark Angel (novel)
    Her Sister's Secret (1947) PRC

Luxury Liner (novel)
    Luxury Liner (1933) PAR

Night Before the Divorce, The (play in collab. L.
Fodor)
    Night Before the Divorce, The (1942) TCF

KAZAN, ELIA

America America (novel)
    America America (1963) WB

Arrangement, The (novel)
    Arrangement, The (1969) WB/SA

KEELER, HARRY STEPHEN

Sing Sing Nights (novel)
    Sing Sing Nights (1935) MON

Twelve Coins of Confucious, The (novel)
    Mysterious Mr. Wong, The (1935) MON

KELLAND, CLARENCE BUDDINGTON

Arizona (novel)
    Arizona (1941) COL

Backbone (story)
    Backbone (1923) G

Cat's Paw, The (story)
    Cat's Paw, The (1934) F

Dance Magic (story)
    Dance Magic (1927) FN

Dreamland (story)
    Strike Me Pink (1936) UA

Face the Facts (story)

119

Mr. Boggs Steps Out (1938) GN

Footlights (novel)
    Speak Easily (1932) MGM

Great Crooner, The (story)
    Mr. Dodd Takes the Air (1937) WB

Miracle (novel)
    Woman's Faith, A (1925) U

Opera Hat (short story)
    Mr. Deeds Goes to Town (1936) COL

Recreation Car (story)
    Florida Special (1936) PAR

Scattergood Baines (stories)
    Scattergood Baines (1941) RKO

Silver Spoon (story)
    Highways by Night (1942) RKO

Stand-In (story)
    Stand-In (1937) UA

Steadfast Heart, The (story)
    Steadfast Heart, The (1923) G

Sugarfoot (novel)
    Sugarfoot (1951) WB

Thirty Day Princess (story)
    Thirty Day Princess (1934) PAR

Valley of the Sun (story)
    Valley of the Sun (1942) RKO

KELLOGG, VIRGINIA

Mary Stevens, M.D. (novel)
    Mary Stevens, M.D. (1933) WB

Road to Reno, The (story)
    Road to Reno, The (1931) PAR

KELLY, GEORGE

Craig's Wife (play)
    Craig's Wife (1928) PAT
    Craig's Wife (1934) MGM
    Harriet Craig (1950) COL

Show-Off, The (play)
    Show-Off, The (1926) PAR
    Show-Off, The (1934) MGM
    Show-Off, The (1947) MGM

Torch Bearers, The (play)
    Doubting Thomas (1935) F

KEROUAC, JACK

Subterraneans, The (novel)
    Subterraneans, The (1960) MGM

KERR, SOPHIE

Big-Hearted Herbert (play)
    Big-Hearted Herbert (1934) WB

Relative Values (story)
    Young Ideas (1924) U

See-Saw (story)
    Invisible Bond, The (1919) PAR

Worldly Goods (novel)
    Worldly Goods (1924) PAR

KESEY, KEN

One Flew Over the Cuckoo's Nest (novel)
    One Flew Over the Kuckoo's Nest (1975) UA

Sometimes a Great Notion (novel)
    Sometimes a Great Notion (1971) U

KESSEL, JOSEPH

Coup de Grace (novel)
    Sirocco (1951) COL

L'Equipage (novel)
    Last Flight, The (1931) FN
    Woman I Love, The (1937) RKO

KESSELRING, JOSEPH

Arsenic and Old Lace (play)
    Arsenic and Old Lace (1944) WB

KEYES, DANIEL

Flowers for Algernon (novel)
    Charly (1968) CRC

KIDDER, EDWARD

Peaceful Valley (play)
    Peaceful Valley (1920) FN

KING, GEORGE S.

Last Slaver, The (novel)
    Slave Ship (1937) TCF

KING, RUFUS

Hidden Hand, The (play)
    Hidden Hand, The (1942) WB

Murder at the Vanities (play in collab. Earl
Carroll)
    Murder at the Vanities (1934) PAR

Secret Beyond the Door (story)
    Secret Beyond the Door (1948) UI

Silent Command, The (story)
    Silent Command, The (1923) F

Victoria Docks at Eight, The (play in collab. C.

Beahan)
      White Tie and Tails (1946) U

KING, STEPHEN

Carrie (novel)
      Carrie (1976) UA

Christine (novel)
      Christine (1983) COL

Cujo (novel)
      Cujo (1983) WB

Dead Zone, The (novel)
      Dead Zone, The (1983) PAR

KINGSLEY, SIDNEY

Dead End (play)
      Dead End (1937) UA

Detective Story (play)
      Detective Story (1951) PAR

Men in White (play)
      Men in White (1934) MGM

KIPLING, RUDYARD

Captains Courageous (novel)
      Captains Courageous (1937) MGM

Gunga Din (poem)
      Gunga Din (1939) RKO

Jungle Books, The (stories)
      Jungle Book (1942) UA
      Jungle Book, The (anim. 1967) BV

Kim (novel)
      Kim (1950) MGM

Light That Failed, The (novel)
      Light That Failed, The (1916) PAT

Light That Failed, The (1923) PAR
Light That Failed, The (1939) PAR

Wee Willie Winkie (novel)
Wee Willie Winkie (1937) TCF

Without Benefit of Clergy (story)
Without Benefit of Clergy (1921) PAT

KLEIN, CHARLES

Gamblers, The (play)
Gamblers, The (1929) WB

Heartease (play)
Heartease (1919) G

Lion and the Mouse, The (play)
Lion and the Mouse, The (1919) VIT
Lion and the Mouse, The (1928) WB

Music Master, The (play)
Music Master, The (1927) F

Potash and Perlmutter (play in collab. Montague Glass)
Potash and Perlmutter (1923) FN

Third Degree, The (play)
Third Degree, The (1927) WB

KLEIN, ERNST

At the End of the World (play)
At the End of the World (1921) PAR

KNIGHT, ERIC

Lassie Come Home (novel)
Lassie Come Home (1943) MGM

This Above All (novel)
This Above All (1942) TCF

KNOBLOCK, EDWARD

Conchita (play)
    Love Comes Along (1930) RKO

Fawn, The (play)
    Marriage Maker (1923) PAR

Kismet (play)
    Kismet (1930) WB
    Kismet (1944) MGM
    Kismet (1955) MGM

Lullaby, The (play)
    Sin of Madelon Claudet, The (1931) MGM

Speakeasy (play in collab. George Rosener)
    Speakeasy (1929) F

KNOWLES, JOHN

Separate Peace, A (novel)
    Separate Peace, A (1972) PAR

KOBER, ARTHUR

Having Wonderful Time (play)
    Having Wonderful Time (1938) RKO

Recipe for Murder (story)
    Great Hotel Murder, The (1935) F

KOONITZ, DEAN R.

Demon Seed (novel)
    Demon Seed (1977) UA

KOPPIT, ARTHUR

Indians (play)
    Buffalo Bill and the Indians (1976) UA

KOSINSKI, JERZY

Being There (novel)
    Being There (1979) UA

KRASNA, NORMAN

Dear Ruth (play)
    Dear Ruth (1947) PAR

John Loves Mary (play)
    John Loves Mary (1949) WB

Kind Sir (play)
    Indiscreet (1958) WB

Mike and Ike (story)
    Big Hangover, The (1950) MGM

Small Miracle (play)
    Four Hours to Kill (1935) PAR

Sunday in New York (play)
    Sunday in New York (1964) MGM

Who Was That Lady? (play)
    Who Was That Lady? (1960) COL

KYNE, PETER B.

All for Love (story)
    Valley of Wanted Men (1935) CONN

Blue Blood and the Pirate (story)
    Breed of the Sea (1926) FBO

Bread on the Waters (short story)
    Hero on Horseback (1927) U

Brothers Under the Skin (short story)
    Brothers Under the Skin (1922) G

Cappy Ricks (short stories)
    Cappy Ricks (1921) PAR

Corn Cob Kelley (story)
    Shamrock Handicap (1926) F

Cornflower Cassie's Concert (short story)
    Beauty and the Bad Man (1925) PDC

Desert of Odyssey (story)
    California (1927) MGM

Dog Meat (short story)
    Blue Blood (1951) MON

Enchanted Hill, The (story)
    Enchanted Hill, The (1925) PAR

Film Star's Holiday, A (story)
    Pride of the Legion (1932) MAS

Great Mono Miracle, The (short story)
    Face in the Fog, A (1936) VIC

Harbor Bar (story)
    Loving Lies (1923) APD

Man's Law (story)
    Self Defense (1933) MON

Never the Twain Shall Meet (story)
    Never the Twain Shall Meet (1925) MG
    Never the Twain Shall Meet (1931) MGM

New Freedom, The (story)
    Men of Action (1935) CONN

Oh, Promise Me (story)
    Buckaree Kid (1926) U
    Flaming Guns (1933) U

On Irish Hill (story)
    Kelly of the Secret Service (1936) VIC

One Eighth Apache (story)
    Danger Ahead (1935) VIC

Parson of Panamint, The (short story)
    Parson of Panamint, The (1916) PAR
    While Satan Sleeps (1922) PAR
    Parson of Panamint, The (1941) PAR

Pride of Palomar, The (short story)

127

Pride of Palomar, The (1922) PAR

Renunciation (story)
    Beautiful Gambler (1921) U

Three Godfathers (novel)
    Three Godfathers (1916) BL
    Hell's Heroes (1929) U
    Three Godfathers (1936) MGM
    Three Godfathers (1948) MGM

Tidy Toreador (story)
    Galloping Fury (1927) U

Understanding Heart, The (novel)
    Understanding Heart, The (1927) MGM

Valley of the Giants (novel)
    Valley of the Giants (1938) WB

L

LAGERLOF, SELMA

Emperor of Portugalia (novel)
        Tower of Lies, The (1925) MG

This Woman and This Man (story)
        Guilty of Love (1920) PAR

Three Who Were Doomed, The (story)
        Three Who Were Doomed, The (1928) MAL

LAIT, JACK

New York Confidential (nonfiction in collab. Lee
Mortimer)
        New York Confidential (1955) WB

One of Us (play)
        Love Burglar, The (1919) PAR

LAKE, STUART N.

Wyatt Earp, Frontier Marshal (novel)
        Frontier Marshal (1934) F
        Frontier Marshal (1939) TCF
        My Darling Clementine (1946) TCF

L'AMOUR, LOUIS

Blackjack Ketchum, Desperado (novel)
    Blackjack Ketchum, Desperado (1956) COL

Broken Gun (novel)
    Cancel My Reservation (1972) WB

Burning Hills, The (novel)
    Burning Hills, The (1956) WB

Heller With a Gun (novel)
    Heller in Pink Tights (1960) PAR

Shalako (novel)
    Shalako (1968) CRC

Taggart (novel)
    Taggart (1964) U

LANDON, MARGARET

Anna and the King of Siam (novel)
    Anna and the King of Siam (1946) TCF
    King and I, The (1956) TCF

LANE, MARK

Rush to Judgment (nonfiction)
    Rush to Judgment (1967) IMP

LARDNER, RING

Alibi Ike (short story)
    Alibi Ike (1935) WB

Big Town, The (short story)
    So This Is New York (1948) UA

Champion (short story)
    Champion (1949) UA

Elmer the Great (play)
    Elmer the Great (1933) FN

Hurry Cane (play in collab. G.M. Cohan)
     Fast Company (1918) BL
     Fast Company (1929) PAR
     Fast Company (1931) MGM
     Fast Company (1953) MGM

June Moon (play in collab. G.S. Kaufman)
     June Moon (1931) PAR
     Blonde Trouble (1937) PAR

New Klondike, The (short story)
     New Klondike, The (1926) PAR

LATIMER, JONATHAN

Dead Don't Care, The (novel)
     Last Warning, The (1938) U

Headed for a Hearse (novel)
     Westland Case, The (1937) U

Lady in the Morgue, The (novel)
     Lady in the Morgue, The (1938) U

LAUMER, KEITH

Deadfall (novel)
     Peeper (1976) TCF

Monitors, The (novel)
     Monitors, The (1969) CUE

LAUREN, S.K.

Distant Fields (play)
     Married and in Love (1940) RKO

Men Must Fight (play in collab. Reginald Lawrence)
     Men Must Fight (1933) MGM

Storks Don't Bring Babies (story)
     My Blue Heaven (1950) TCF

LAURENTS, ARTHUR

Gypsy (play)
    Gypsy (1962) WB

Home of the Brave (play)
    Home of the Brave (1949) UA

Time of the Cuckoo, The (play)
    Summertime (1955) UA

West Side Story (play in collab. L. Bernstein)
    West Side Story (1961) UA

LAWES, LEWIS E.

Chalked Out (play in collab. Jonathan Finn)
    You Can't Get Away With Murder (1939) WB

Twenty Thousand Years in Sing Sing (nonfiction)
    Twenty Thousand Years in Sing Sing (1933) FN
    Invisible Stripes (1940) WB
    Castle on the Hudson (1940) WB

LAWRENCE, D.H.

Fox, The (novel)
    Fox, The (1968) CLARIDGE PICT.

LAWRENCE, JEROME

First Monday in October (play in collab. R.E. Lee)
    First Monday in October (1981) PAR

Inherit the Wind (play in collab. R.E. Lee)
    Inherit the Wind (1960) UA

LAWRENCE, JOSEPHINE

Years Are So Long, The (novel)
    Make Way for Tomorrow (1937) PAR

LAWSON, JOHN HOWARD

Success Story (play)
    Success at Any Price (1934) RKO

LE BLANC, MAURICE

Arsene Lupin (play in collab. F. de Croisset)
    Arsene Lupin (1932) MGM

LE CARRE, JOHN

Call for the Dead (novel)
    Deadly Affair, The (1966) COL

Spy Who Came in From the Cold, The (novel)
    Spy Who Came in From the Cold, The (1965) PAR

LEE, HARPER

To Kill a Mockingbird (novel)
    To Kill a Mockingbird (1962) U

LEE, ROBERT E.

First Monday in October (play in collab. J.
Lawrence)
    First Monday in October (1981) PAR

Inherit the Wind (play in collab. J. Lawrence)
    Inherit the Wind (1960) UA

LEIBER, FRITZ

Conjure Wife (novel)
    Burn Witch Burn (1962) AI

LERNER, ALAN JAY

Brigadoon (play)
    Brigadoon (1954) MGM

Camelot (play)

        Camelot (1967) WB/SA

My Fair Lady (play in collab. F. Loewe; from Shaw's
Pygmalion)
        My Fair Lady (1965) WB

LEROUX, GASTON

Balaoo (play)
        Wizard, The (1927) F

Phantom of the Opera, The (novel)
        Phantom of the Opera, The (1925) U
        Phantom of the Opera, The (1943) U

LEVIN, IRA

Critic's Choice (play)
        Critic's Choice (1963) WB

Deathtrap (play)
        Deathtrap (1982) WB

No Time for Sergeants (play)
        No Time for Sergeants (1958) WB

Rosemary's Baby (novel)
        Rosemary's Baby (1968) PAR

Stepford Wives, The (novel)
        Stepford Wives, The (1975) COL

LEVIN, MEYER

Compulsion (novel)
        Compulsion (1959) TCF

LEWIS, SINCLAIR

Angela Is 22 (play in collab. Fay Wray)
        This Is the Life (1944) U

Ann Vickers (novel)
        Ann Vickers (1933) RKO

Arrowsmith (novel)
    Arrowsmith (1933) G

Babbitt (novel)
    Babbitt (1924) WB
    Babbitt (1934) FN

Cass Timberlane (novel)
    Cass Timberlane (1947) MGM

Dodsworth (novel)
    Dodsworth (1936) UA

Elmer Gantry (novel)
    Elmer Gantry (1960) UA

Let's Play King (novel)
    Newly Rich (1931) PAR

Main Street (novel)
    Main Street (1923) WB
    I Married a Doctor (1936) WB

LINDSAY, HOWARD

Anything Goes (play in collab. Russell Crouse)
    Anything Goes (1936) PAR
    Anything Goes (1956) PAR

Call Me Madam (play in collab. Russell Crouse)
    Call Me Madam (1953) TCF

Life With Father (play in collab. Russell Crouse)
    Life With Father (1947) WB

Oh, Promise Me (play in collab. Bertram Robinson)
    Love, Honor and Oh, Baby! (1933) U

She Loves Me Not (play)
    She Loves Me Not (1934) PAR
    True to the Army (1942) PAR

Slight Case of Murder, A (play in collab. D.
Runyon)
    Slight Case of Murder, A (1938) WB
    Stop, You're Killing Me (1952) WB

Sound of Music, The (play)
    Sound of Music, The (1965) TCF

State of the Union (play in collab. Russell Crouse)
    State of the Union (1948) MGM

Tall Story (play in collab. Russell Crouse)
    Tall Story (1960) WB

Tommy (play in collab. Bertram Robinson)
    She's My Weakness (1930) RKO

Your Uncle Dudley (play in collab. Bertram
Robinson)
        Your Uncle Dudley (1935) F

LLEWELLYN, RICHARD

How Green Was My Valley (novel)
    How Green Was My Valley (1941) TCF

None But the Lonely Heart (novel)
    None But the Lonely Heart (1944) RKO

LOCKE, WILLIAM J.

Coming of Amos, The (novel)
    Coming of Amos, The (1925) PDC

Idols (novel)
    Oath, The (1921) FN

Mountebank, The (novel)
    Side Show of Life, The (1924) PAR

Shorn Lamb, The (novel)
    Strangers in Love (1932) PAR

Simon the Jester (novel)
    Simon the Jester (1925) PDC

LOCKRIDGE, ROSS

Raintree County (novel)
    Raintree County (1957) MGM

LOGAN, JOSHUA

Higher and Higher (play in collab. Gladys Hurlbut)
    Higher and Higher (1944) RKO

Mister Roberts (play in collab. Thomas Heggen)
    Mister Roberts (1955) WB

LONDON, JACK

Abysmal Brute, The (short story)
    Conflict (1921) U
    Abysmal Brute, The (1923) U
    Conflict (1937) U

Adventure (story)
    Adventure (1925) PAR

Burning Daylight (story)
    Burning Daylight (1914) PAR
    Burning Daylight (1920) M
    Burning Daylight (1928) FN

Call of the Wild (novel)
    Call of the Wild (1923) PAT
    Call of the Wild (1935) TC

Demetrios Contos (story)
    Devil's Skipper, The (1928) TIF

Flush of Gold (story)
    Alaska (1944) MON

Gold Hunters of the North (short story)
    North to the Klondike (1942) U

John Barleycorn (nonfiction)
    John Barleycorn (1914) PAR

Little Lady of the Big House (story)
    Little Fool (1921) M

Martin Eden (novel)
    Adventures of Martin Eden, The (1942) COL

Mexican, The (story)
    Fighter, The (1952) UA

Romance of the Redwoods (story)
    Romance of the Redwoods (1939) COL

Sea Wolf, The (novel)
    Sea Wolf, The (1920) PAR
    Sea Wolf, The (1925) INC
    Sea Wolf, The (1930) F
    Sea Wolf, The (1941) WB
    Wolf Larsen (1958) AA

White and Yellow (story)
    Haunted Ship, The (1928)TIF

White Fang (novel)
    White Fang (1936) TCF

Yellow Handkerchief, The (short story)
    Stormy Waters (1928) TIF

LONG, JOHN LUTHER

Madame Butterfly (novel)
    Madame Butterfly (1915) PAR
    Madame Butterfly (1932) PAR

LONGFELLOW, HENRY WADSWORTH

Courtship of Myles Standish, The (poem)
    Courtship of Myles Standish, The (1923) AE

Evangeline (poem)
    Evangeline (1919) F
    Evangeline (1929) UA

Hiawatha (poem)
    Hiawatha (1952) MON

Village Blacksmith, The (poem)
    Village Blacksmith, The (1922) F

Wreck of the Hesperus, The (poem)
    Wreck of the Hesperus, The (1927) PAT

LONSDALE, FREDERICK

Aren't We All? (play)
      Kiss in the Dark, A (1925) PAR
      Aren't We All? (1932) PAR

High Road, The (play)
      Lady of Scandal, The (1930) MGM

Last of Mrs. Cheyney, The (play)
      Last of Mrs. Cheyney, The (1929) MGM
      Last of Mrs. Cheyney, The (1937) MGM
      Law and the Lady, The (1951) MGM

Spring Cleaning (play)
      Fast Set, The (1924) PAR

LOOS, ANITA

Ada Beats the Drum (story)
      Mama Steps Out (1937) MGM

But Gentlemen Marry Brunettes (play)
      Gentlemen Marry Brunettes (1955) UA

Gentlemen Prefer Blondes (novel)
      Gentlemen Prefer Blondes (1928) PAR
      Gentlemen Prefer Blondes (1953) TCF

LOUDEN, THOMAS

Champion (play in collab. A.E. Thomas)
      World's Champion (1922) PAR

LOVECRAFT, H.P.

Colour Out of Space (short story)
      Die, Monster, Die (1965) AI

Dunwich Horror, The (short story)
      Dunwich Horror, The (1970) AI

LUDLUM, ROBERT

Osterman Weekend, The (novel)
      Osterman Weekend, The (1983) TCF

M

MAAS, PETER

King of the Gypsies (novel)
    King of the Gypsies (1978) PAR

Serpico (novel)
    Serpico (1973) PAR

MacARTHUR, CHARLES

Front Page, The (play in collab. B. Hecht)
    Front Page, The (1931) UA
    His Girl Friday (1940) COL
    Front Page, The (1974) U

Jumbo (play in collab. B. Hecht)
    Jumbo (1962) MGM

Ladies and Gentlemen (play in collab. B. Hecht)
    Perfect Strangers (1950) WB

Lulu Belle (play in collab. E. Sheldon)
    Lulu Belle (1948) COL

Twentieth Century (play in collab. B. Hecht)
    Twentieth Century (1934) COL
    Streamline Express (1935) MAS

McCARTHY, JUSTIN HUNTLEY

Fighting O'Flynn, The (story)
    Fighting O'Flynn, The (1949) UI

If I Were King (novel, play)
    If I Were King (1920) F
    Vagabond King, The (1930) PAR
    If I Were King (1938) PAR
    Vagabond King, The (1956) PAR

McCARTHY, MARY

Group, The (novel)
    Group, The (1966) UA

McCULLERS, CARSON

Heart Is a Lonely Hunter, The (novel)
    Heart Is a Lonely Hunter, The (1968) WB/SA

Member of the Wedding, The (novel, play)
    Member of the Wedding, The (1952) COL

Reflections in a Golden Eye (novel)
    Reflections in a Golden Eye (1967) WB/SA

McCULLEY, JOHNSTON

Curse of Capistrano, The (novel)
    Mark of Zorro, The (1920) UA
    Mark of Zorro, The (1940) TCF
    Sign of Zorro, The (1961) BV

Don Peon (story)
    California Conquest (1951) COL

Ice Flood, The (story)
    Ice Flood, The (1926) U

MacDONALD, JOHN D.

Darker Than Amber (novel)
    Darker Than Amber (1970) NG

Executioners, The (novel)
    Cape Fear (1962) UI

MacDONALD, PHILIP

Escape (story)
    Nightmare (1942) U

Hour of 13, The (novel)
    Hour of 13, The (1952) MGM

List of Adrian Messenger, The (novel)
    List of Adrian Messenger, The (1963) U

Mystery of the Dead Police (novel)
    Mystery of Mr. X, The (1934) MGM

Patrol (novel)
    Lost Patrol, The (1934) RKO

Warrant for X (novel)
    Twenty-Three Paces to Baker Street (1956) TCF

MacDONALD, ROSS

Drowning Pool, The (novel)
    Drowning Pool, The (1975) WB

Moving Target, The (novel)
    Harper (1966) WB

McGIVERN, WILLIAM P.

Caper of the Golden Bulls, The (novel)
    Caper of the Golden Bulls, The (1967) EMB

Darkest Hour, The (novel)
    Hell on Frisco Bay (1956) WB

Odds Against Tomorrow (novel)
    Odds Against Tomorrow (1959) UA

Rogue Cop (novel)
    Rogue Cop (1954) MGM

MacGUIRE, DON

Bad Time at Hondo (novel)
    Bad Day at Black Rock (1955) MGM

Damon and Pythias (story)
    Delicate Delinquent, The (1957) PAR

MacLEAN, ALISTAIR

Guns of Navarone, The (novel)
    Guns of Navarone, The (1961) COL

Ice Station Zebra (novel)
    Ice Station Zebra (1968) MGM

Secret Ways, The (novel)
    Secret Ways, The (1961) UI

Where Eagles Dare (novel)
    Where Eagles Dare (1969) MGM

McMANUS, GEORGE

Bringing Up Father (comic strip)
    Bringing Up Father (1928) MGM
    Bringing Up Father (1946) MON

McMURTRY, LARRY

Horseman, Pass By (novel)
    Hud (1963) PAR

Last Picture Show, The (novel)
    Last Picture Show, The (1971) COL

Leaving Cheyenne (novel)
    Lovin' Molly (1974) COL

Terms of Endearment (novel)
    Terms of Endearment (1983) PAR

143

McNEILE, H.C.

Bulldog Drummond (novel)
    Bulldog Drummond's Bride (1939) PAR

Bulldog Drummond (play)
    Bulldog Drummond (1929) UA

Challenge (novel)
    Bulldog Drummond in Africa (1938) PAR

Female of the Species (novel)
    Bulldog Drummond Comes Back (1937) PAR

Final Count, The (novel)
    Arrest Bulldog Drummond (1939) PAR

Third Round, The (novel)
    Bulldog Drummond's Peril (1938) PAR

MAETERLINCK, MAURICE

Blue Bird, The (play)
    Blue Bird, The (1918) ART
    Blue Bird, The (1940) TCF

MAIBAUM, RICHARD

See My Lawyer (play in collab. H. Clork)
    See My Lawyer (1945) U

Sweet Mystery of Life (play)
    Gold Diggers of 1937 (1936) WB

MAILER, NORMAN

American Dream, An (novel)
    American Dream, An (1966) WB

Naked and the Dead, The (novel)
    Naked and the Dead, The (1958) WB

MAJOR, CHARLES

When Knighthood Was in Flower (novel)
    When Knighthood Was in Flower (1922) PAR
    Sword and the Rose (1953) RKO

Yolanda (novel)
    Yolanda (1924) MG

MALAMUD, BERNARD

Angel Levine, The (short story)
    Angel Levine, The (1970) UA

Fixer, The (novel)
    Fixer, The (1968) MGM

MALLORY, JAY (Joyce Carey)

Sweet Aloes (play)
    Give Me Your Heart (1936) WB

MALORY, SIR THOMAS

Morte D'Arthur (poem)
    Knights of the Round Table (1953) MGM

MALTZ, ALBERT

Merry-Go-Round (play in collab. George Sklar)
    Afraid to Talk (1932) U

MANKIEWICZ, DON M.

Trial (novel)
    Trial (1955) MGM

MANNERS, J. HARTLEY

Gay Divorcee, The (play)
    Gay Divorcee, The (1934) RKO

Happiness (play)
    Happiness (1924) MG

National Anthem, The (play)
    Marriage Whirl, The (1925) FN

Peg o' My Heart (play)
    Peg o' My Heart (1922) M
    Peg o' My Heart (1933) MGM

MARASCO, ROBERT

Child's Play (play)
    Child's Play (1972) PAR

MARCH, WILLIAM

Bad Seed, The (novel)
    Bad Seed, The (1956) WB

MARQUAND, JOHN P.

B.F.'s Daughter (novel)
    B.F.'s Daughter (1948) MGM

H.M. Pulham, Esq. (novel)
    H.M. Pulham, Esq. (1941) MGM

Late George Apley, The (play in collab. G.S.
Kaufman)
    Late George Apley, The (1947) TCF

Melville Goodwin, U.S.A. (novel)
    Top Secret Affair (1957) WB

Stopover Tokyo (novel)
    Stopover Tokyo (1957) TCF

MARQUIS, DON

Archy and Mehitabel (stories)
    Shinbone Alley (anim. 1971) AA

Old Soak, The (story)
    Good Old Soak (1937) MGM

MASON, A.E.W.

Four Feathers (novel)
    Four Feathers (1929) PAR

Green Stockings (play)
    Green Stockings (1915) VIT
    Flirting Widow, The (1930) FN

Widow From Monte Carlo, The (play in collab. Ian
Hay)
    Widow From Monte Carlo, The (1930) WB

Witness for the Defense, The (play)
    Witness for the Defense, The (1919) PAR

MATHESON, RICHARD

Bid Time Return (novel)
    Somewhere in Time (1980) U

Hell House (novel)
    Legend of Hell House, The (1973) TCF

Omega Man, The (novel)
    Omega Man, The (1971) WB

Shrinking Man, The (novel)
    Incredible Shrinking Man, The (1957) U

MAUGHAM, W. SOMERSET

Caesar's Wife (play)
    Infatuation (1926) FN

Christmas Holiday (novel)
    Christmas Holiday (1944) U

Circle, The (play)
    Circle, The (1925) MG
    Strictly Unconventional (1930) MGM

Constant Wife, The (short story)
    Charming Sinners (1929) PAR

147

East of Suez (play)
    East of Suez (1925) PAR

Hour Before the Dawn, The (novel)
    Hour Before the Dawn, The (1944) PAR

Land of Promise, The (play)
    Canadian, The (1926) PAR

Letter, The (play)
    Letter, The (1929) PAR
    Letter, The (1940) WB

Magician, The (story)
    Magician, The (1926) MGM

Moon and Sixpence, The (novel)
    Moon and Sixpence, The (1942) UA

Narrow Corner, The (novel)
    Narrow Corner, The (1933) WB

Of Human Bondage (novel)
    Of Human Bondage (1934) RKO
    Of Human Bondage (1946) WB
    Of Human Bondage (1964) MGM/SA

Our Betters (play)
    Our Betters (1933) RKO

Painted Veil, The (novel)
    Painted Veil, The (1934) MGM
    Seventh Sin, The (1957) MGM

Razor's Edge, The (novel)
    Razor's Edge, The (1946) TCF
    Razor's Edge, The (1985)

Sacred Flame, The (play)
    Sacred Flame, The (1929) WB
    Right to Live, The (1935) WB

Sadie Thompson (story)
    Sadie Thompson (1928) UA
    Rain (1932) UA
    Miss Sadie Thompson (1954) COL

Three in Eden (short story)

        Isle of Fury (1936) WB

Too Many Husbands (play)
        Too Many Husbands (1940) COL
        Three for the Show (1955) COL

MAULDIN, BILL

Up Front (novel)
        Up Front (1951) UI

MAUPASSANT, GUY DE

Le Rosier de Madame (short story)
        He (1933) ASTOR

Private Affairs of Bel Ami, The (novel)
        Private Affairs of Bel Ami, The (1947) UA

MAURETTE, MARCELLE

Anastasia (play)
        Anastasia (1956) TCF

MAXIM, HUDSON

Defenseless America (novel)
        Battle Cry for Peace, The (1915) VIT

MAYO, MARGARET

Baby Mine (play)
        Baby Mine (1917) G
        Baby Mine (1928) MGM

Polly of the Circus (play)
        Polly of the Circus (1917) G
        Polly of the Circus (1932) MGM

Twin Beds (play in collab. Salisbury Field)
        Twin Beds (1920) FN
        Twin Beds (1929) FN
        Twin Beds (1942) UA

MEAD, SHEPHERD

How to Succeed in Business Without Really Trying
(novel)
      How to Succeed in Business Without Really
      Trying (1967) UA

MEDOFF, MARK

When You Comin' Back, Red Ryder? (play)
      When You Comin' Back, Red Ryder? (1979) COL

MELVILLE, HERMAN

Billy Budd (novel)
      Billy Budd (1962) AA

Moby Dick (novel)
      Sea Beast, The (1926) WB
      Moby Dick (1930) WB
      Moby Dick (1956) WB

Typee (novel)
      Enchanted Island (1929) U

MERIMEE, PROSPER

Carmen
      Carmen (1915) PAR
      Carmen (1915) F
      Carmen (1916) ESSANAY
      Loves of Carmen (1927) F
      Loves of Carmen, The (1948) COL

Colomba (story)
      Vendetta (1950) RKO

MERRITT, ABRAHAM A.

Burn, Witch, Burn (novel)
      Devil-Doll, The (1936) MGM

METALIOUS, GRACE

Peyton Place (novel)
    Peyton Place (1957) TCF

Return to Peyton Place (novel)
    Return to Peyton Place (1961) TCF

MICHENER, JAMES A.

Bridges at Toko-Ri, The (novel)
    Bridges at Toko-Ri, The (1955) PAR

Caravans (novel)
    Caravans (1978) U

Forgotten Heroes of Korea, The (article)
    Men of the Fighting Lady (1954) MGM

Hawaii (novel)
    Hawaii (1966) UA
    Hawaiians, The (1970) UA

Return to Paradise (novel)
    Return to Paradise (1953) UA

Sayonara (novel)
    Sayonara (1957) WB

Tales of the South Pacific (short stories)
    South Pacific (1956) TCF

Until They Sail (short story)
    Until They Sail (1957) MGM

MILES, RICHARD

That Cold Day in the Park (novel)
    That Cold Day in the Park (1969) CUE

MILLER, ALICE D.

Adventuress (story)
    Keyhole, The (1933) WB

Charm School (novel)

Someone to Love (1928) PAR

Come Out of the Kitchen (novel in collab. A.E.
Thomas)
    Come Out of the Kitchen (1919) PAR
    Honey (1930) PAR

Gowns by Roberta (novel)
    Roberta (1935) RKO

Ladies Must Live (novel)
    Ladies Must Live (1921) PAR

Manslaughter (novel)
    Manslaughter (1922) PAR
    Manslaughter (1930) PAR

White Cliffs, The (poem)
    White Cliffs of Dover, The (1944) MGM

MILLER, ARTHUR

All My Sons (play)
    All My Sons (1948) UI

Death of a Salesman (play)
    Death of a Salesman (1951) COL

View From the Bridge, A (play)
    View From the Bridge, A (1962) CDI

MILLER, HENRY

Tropic of Cancer (novel)
    Tropic of Cancer (1970) PAR

MILLER, JASON

That Championship Season (play)
    That Championship Season (1982) CANNON

MILNE, A.A.

Dover Road (novel)

152

```
        Little Adventuress (1927) PDC
        Where Sinners Meet (1934) RKO


MITCHELL, MARGARET

Gone With the Wind (novel)
        Gone With the Wind (1939) MGM


MOLNAR, FERENC

Fashions for Men (play)
        Fine Clothes (1925) UA

Girl From Trieste, The (play)
        Bride Wore Red, The (1937) MGM

Good Fairy, The (play)
        Good Fairy, The (1935) U
        I'll Be Yours (1947) U

Great Love (play)
        Double Wedding (1937) MGM

Guardsman, The (play)
        Guardsman, The (1927) MGM
        Guardsman, The (1931) MGM
        Chocolate Soldier, The (1941) MGM

Liliom (play)
        Liliom (1930) F
        Carousel (1956) TCF

Olympia (play)
        His Glorious Night (1929) MGM
        Breath of Scandal, A (1960) PAR

Paul Street Boys, The (novel)
        No Greater Glory (1934) COL

Swan, The (play)
        Swan, The (1925) PAR
        One Romantic Night (1930) UA
        Swan, The (1956) MGM

Woman With the Mask (play)
        Masked Dancer (1924) PRINCIPAL
```

153

MONTAGUE, MARGARET PRESCOTT

Uncle Sam of Freedom Ridge (short story)
    Uncle Sam of Freedom Ridge (1920) LEM

MONTGOMERY, L.M.

Anne of the Green Gables (novel)
    Anne of the Green Gables (1919) REA
    Anne of the Green Gables (1934) RKO

Anne of the Windy Poplars (novel)
    Anne of the Windy Poplars (1940) RKO

MOODY, RALPH

Little Britches (novel)
    Wild Country, The (1971) BV

MOODY, WILLIAM VAUGHN

Faith Healer, The (play)
    Faith Healer, The (1921) PAR

Great Divide, The (play)
    Great Divide, The (1915) PAR
    Great Divide, The (1925) MG
    Woman Hungry (1931) FN

MOORE, ROBIN

French Connection, The (novel)
    French Connection, The (1971) TCF

MORLEY, CHRISTOPHER

Kitty Foyle (novel)
    Kitty Foyle (1940) RKO

MORRIS, GOUVERNEUR

Behind the Door (novel)
    Behind the Door (1920) PAR

Better Wife, A (novel)
    Anybody's Woman (1930) PAR

Man Who Played God, The (novel)
    Man Who Played God, The (1932) WB

Purple Mask (novel)
    Ace of Hearts (1921) G

Right to Live, The (novel)
    That Model From Paris (1926) TIF

MULFORD, CLARENCE

Bar 20 - Three (novel)
    Three on the Trail (1936) PAR

Bring Me His Ears (story)
    Borderland (1937) PAR

Cottonwood Gulch (story)
    North of the Rio Grande (1937) PAR

Hopalong Cassidy Returns (novel)
    Eagle's Brood, The (1935) PAR

Orphan, The (novel)
    Deadwood Coach, The (1925) F

Round-Up, The (story)
    Hills of Old Wyoming (1937) PAR

155

N

NABOKOV, VLADIMIR

Lolita (novel)
    Lolita (1962) MGM

NASH, OGDEN

Tinted Venus, The (play in collab. S.J. Perelman)
    One Touch of Venus (1948) U

NASH, RICHARD

Rainmaker, The (play)
    Rainmaker, The (1956) PAR

NATHAN, ROBERT

Bishop's Wife, The (novel)
    Bishop's Wife, The (1947) RKO

Enchanted Voyage, The (novel)
    Wake Up and Dream (1946) TCF

One More Spring (novel)
    One More Spring (1935) F

Portrait of Jennie (novel)
      Portrait of Jennie (1949) SEZ

NEUMANN, ALFRED

Patriot, The (play)
      Patriot, The (1928) PAR

NICHOLS, ANNE

Abie's Irish Rose (play)
      Abie's Irish Rose (1928) PAR
      Abie's Irish Rose (1946) UA

Give Me a Sailor (play)
      Give Me a Sailor (1938) PAR

Just Married (play)
      Just Married (1928) PAR

Love-Dreams (play in collab. Elmer Harris)
      Her Gilded Cage (1922) PAR

NICHOLS, JOHN

Sterile Cuckoo, The (novel)
      Sterile Cuckoo, The (1969) PAR

NICHOLSON, KENYON

Barker, The (play)
      Barker, The (1928) FN
      Hoopla (1933) F

Blind Spot (play)
      Taxi (1932) WB

Sailor Beware (play)
      Lady, Be Careful (1936) PAR
      Fleet's In, The (1942) PAR
      Sailor Beware (1952) PAR

Swing Your Lady (play in collab. Charles Robinson)
      Swing Your Lady (1938) PAR

157

Torch Song, The (play)
    Laughing Sinners (1931) MGM

Waterfront (play)
    Waterfront (1939) WB

NORDHOFF, CHARLES

Botany Bay (novel in collab. James N. Hall)
    Botany Bay (1953) PAR

High Barbaree (novel in collab. James N. Hall)
    High Barbaree (1947) MGM

Hurricane, The (novel in collab. James N. Hall)
    Hurricane, The (1937) UA
    Hurricane (1979) PAR

Mutiny on the Bounty (novel in collab. James N. Hall)
    Mutiny on the Bounty (1935) MGM
    Mutiny on the Bounty (1962) MGM

No More Gas (novel in collab. James N. Hall)
    Tuttles of Tahiti, The (1942) RKO

NORRIS, FRANK

McTeague (novel)
    Greed (1924) MG

Moran of the Lady Letty (short story)
    Moran of the Lady Letty (1922) PAR

NORRIS, KATHLEEN

Callahans and the Murphys, The (novel)
    Callahans and the Murphys, The (1927) MGM

Christine of the Hungry Heart (novel)
    Christine of the Hungry Heart (1924) FN

Flaming Passion (novel)
    Lucretia Lombard (1923) WB

158

Manhattan Love Song (novel)
    Change of Heart (1934) F

Mother (novel)
    Mother (1927) FBO

My Best Girl (story)
    My Best Girl (1927) UA

Navy Wife (story)
    Beauty's Daughter (1935) F

Passion Flower (novel)
    Passion Flower (1930) MGM

Rose of the World (novel)
    Rose of the World (1925) WB

Second Hand Wife (novel)
    Second Hand Wife (1933) F

Sisters (novel)
    Sisters (1922) AR

Walls of Gold (novel)
    Walls of Gold (1933) F

NOVELLO, IVOR

Truth Game, The (play)
    But the Flesh Is Weak (1932) MGM
    Free and Easy (1941) MGM

NOYES, ALFRED E.

Dick Turpin's Ride (poem)
    Lady and the Bandit, The (1951) COL

Highwayman, The (poem)
    Highwayman, The (1951) AA

NUGENT, ELLIOTT

Father's Day (play in collab. J.C. Nugent)

Richest Man in the World (1930) MGM

Kempy (play in collab. J.C. Nugent)
     Wise Girls (1930) MGM

Male Animal, The (play)
     Male Animal, The (1942) WB
     She's Working Her Way Through College (1952)
     WB

Poor Nut, The (play in collab. J.C. Nugent)
     Poor Nut, The (1927) FN
     Local Boy Makes Good (1931) FN

NYITRAY, EMIL

No, No, Nanette (play in collab. with others)
     No, No, Nanette (1930) FN
     No, No, Nanette (1940) RKO
     Tea for Two (1950) WB

O

O'CASEY, SEAN

Plough and the Stars, The (play)
     Plough and the Stars, The (1937) RKO

O'CONNOR, EDWIN

Last Hurrah, The (novel)
     Last Hurrah, The (1958) COL

O'CONNOR, FLANNERY

Wise Blood (novel)
     Wise Blood (1980) NEW LINE

ODETS, CLIFFORD

Big Knife, The (play)
     Big Knife, The (1955) UA

Clash by Night (play)
     Clash by Night (1952) RKO

Country Girl, The (play)
     Country Girl, The (1954) PAR

Golden Boy (play)
    Golden Boy (1939) COL

O'FLAHERTY, LIAM

Informer, The (novel)
    Informer, The (1935) RKO
    Up Tight (1968) PAR

O'HARA, JOHN

Butterfield 8 (novel)
    Butterfield 8 (1960) MGM

From the Terrace (novel)
    From the Terrace (1960) TCF

Rage to Live, A (novel)
    Rage to Live, A (1965) UA

Ten North Frederick (novel)
    Ten North Frederick (1958) TCF

O'NEILL, EUGENE

Ah, Wilderness! (play)
    Ah, Wilderness! (1935) MGM
    Summer Holiday (1948) MGM

Anna Christie (play)
    Anna Christie (1923) FN
    Anna Christie (1930) MGM

Bound East for Cardiff (one-act play)
    Long Voyage Home, The (1940) UA

Desire Under the Elms (play)
    Desire Under the Elms (1958) PAR

Emperor Jones, The (play)
    Emperor Jones, The (1933) UA

Hairy Ape, The (play)
    Hairy Ape, The (1944) UA

162

Iceman Cometh, The (play)
    Iceman Cometh, The (1973) AFT

In the Zone (one-act play)
    Long Voyage Home, The (1940) UA

Long Day's Journey Into Night (play)
    Long Day's Journey Into Night (1962) EMB

Long Voyage Home, The (one-act play)
    Long Voyage Home, The (1940) UA

Moon of the Caribbees, The (one-act play)
    Long Voyage Home, The (1940) UA

Mourning Becomes Electra (play)
    Mourning Becomes Electra (1947) RKO

Strange Interlude (play)
    Strange Interlude (1932) MGM

OPPENHEIM, E. PHILLIPPS

Ex-Duke, The (novel)
    Prince of Tempters, The (1926) FN

Great Impersonation, The (novel)
    Great Impersonation, The (1921) PAR
    Great Impersonation, The (1935) U
    Great Impersonation, The (1942) U

Hillman, The (novel)
    Behold This Woman (1924) VIT

Inevitable Millionaire, The (novel)
    Millionaires (1926) WB

Jeanne and the Marshes (novel)
    Behind Masks (1932) COL

Malefactor, The (novel)
    Test of Honor, The (1919) PAR

Tempting of Tavernake (story)
    Sisters of Eve (1928) RAYART

ORCZY, BARONESS

Emperor's Candlesticks, The (novel)
    Emperor's Candlesticks, The (1937) MGM

I Will Repay (novel)
    Swords and the Woman (1924) FBO

Leatherface (novel)
    Two Loves (1928) UA

ORR, MARY

Wallflower (play in collab. Reginald Denham)
    Wallflower (1948) WB

Wisdom of Eve, The (short story)
    All About Eve (1950) TCF

OSBORN, JR., JOHN JAY

Paper Chase, The (novel)
    Paper Chase, The (1973) TCF

OSBORN, PAUL

On Borrowed Time (play based on L.E. Watkin's
novel)
    On Borrowed Time (1939) MGM

Vinegar Tree, The (play)
    Should Ladies Behave? (1933) MGM

World of Suzie Wong, The (play)
    World of Suzie Wong, The (1960) PAR

OSBORNE, HUBERT

Shore Leave (play)
    Shore Leave (1925) FN
    Follow the Fleet (1936) RKO
    Hit the Deck (1955) MGM

OTIS, JAMES

Toby Tyler (novel)
    Circus Days (1923) FN
    Toby Tyler (1960) BV

OUIDA

Dog of Flanders, A (novel)
    Boy of Flanders, A (1924) MG
    Dog of Flanders, A (1960) TCF

Under Two Flags (novel)
    Under Two Flags (1916) F
    Under Two Flags (1922) U
    Under Two Flags (1936) TCF

OURSLER, FULTON

All the King's Men (play)
    Second Wife (1930) RKO
    Second Wife (1936) RKO

Great Jasper, The (novel)
    Great Jasper, The (1933) RKO

Spider, The (play in collab. Lowell Brentano)
    Spider, The (1931) F

P

PACKARD, FRANK L.

Miracle Man, The (novel, play)
    Miracle Man, The (1919) PAR
    Miracle Man, The (1932) PAR

Sin That Was His, The (novel)
    Sin That Was His, The (1920) SEZ

PAGE, ELIZABETH

Tree of Liberty, The (novel)
    Howards of Virginia, The (1940) COL

PAGNOL, MARCEL

Fanny (play)
    Port of Seven Seas (1938) MGM
    Fanny (1961) WB

Topaze (play)
    Topaze (1933) RKO

PALMER, STUART

Murder on a Bridal Path (novel)

166

Murder on a Bridal Path (1936) RKO

Murder on a Honeymoon (novel)
Murder on a Honeymoon (1935) RKO

Murder on the Blackboard (novel)
Murder on the Blackboard (1934) RKO

Penguin Pool Murder, The (novel)
Penguin Pool Murder, The (1932) RKO

Riddle of the Dangling Pearls, The (novel)
Plot Thickens, The (1936) RKO

PARKER, LOTTIE BLAIR

Way Down East (play)
Way Down East (1920) UA
Way Down East (1935) F

PARKS, GORDON

Learning Tree, The (novel)
Learning Tree, The (1969) WB/SA

PASCAL, ERNEST

Age for Love, The (play)
Age for Love, The (1931) UA

Charlatan, The (play in collab. Leonard Praskins)
Charlatan, The (1929) U

Dark Swan, The (novel)
Dark Swan, The (1924) WB
Wedding Rings (1930) FN

Egypt (novel)
Sensation Seekers (1927) U

Hell's Highroad (story)
Hell's Highroad (1925) PDC

King's Vacation, The (story)
King's Vacation, The (1933) WB

167

Marriage Bed, The (play)
     Husband's Holiday (1931) PAR

PASTERNAK, BORIS

Doctor Zhivago (novel)
     Doctor Zhivago (1965) MGM

PATON, ALAN

Cry the Beloved Country (novel)
     Lost in the Stars (1974) AFT

PATRICK, JOHN

Hasty Heart, The (play)
     Hasty Heart, The (1950) WB

Teahouse of the August Moon, The (play from V.
Sneider's novel)
     Teahouse of the August Moon, The (1956) MGM

PEARCE, DONN

Cool Hand Luke (novel)
     Cool Hand Luke (1967) WB

PECK, GEORGE W.

Peck's Bad Boy (novel)
     Peck's Bad Boy (1921) FN
     Peck's Bad Boy (1934) F

PERELMAN, S.J.

All Good Americans (play in collab. Laura Perelman)
     Paris Interlude (1934) MGM

Night Before Christmas, The (play in collab. Laura
Perelman)
     Larceny, Inc. (1942) WB

Tinted Venus, The (play in collab. O. Nash)
    One Touch of Venus (1948) U

PERRAULT, CHARLES

Cinderella (fairy tale)
    Cinderella (1914) PAR
    Cinderella (anim. 1950) RKO

Sleeping Beauty (fairy tale)
    Sleeping Beauty (anim. 1959) BV

PERRY, GEORGE SESSIONS

Hold Autumn in Your Hand (novel)
    Southerner, The (1945) UA

PINERO, ARTHUR WING

Enchanted Cottage, The (play)
    Enchanted Cottage, The (1924) FN
    Enchanted Cottage, The (1945) RKO

His House in Order (play)
    His House in Order (1920) PAR

Trelawney of the Wells (play)
    Actress, The (1928) MGM

PINERO, MIGUEL

Short Eyes (play)
    Short Eyes (1977) PAR

PINTER, HAROLD

Homecoming, The (play)
    Homecoming, The (1973) AFT

PIRANDELLO, LUIGI

169

As Before, Better Than Before (play)
    This Love of Ours (1945) U
    Never Say Goodbye (1956) UI

As You Desire Me (play)
    As You Desire Me (1932) MGM

PLATH, SYLVIA

Bell Jar, The (novel)
    Bell Jar, The (1979) AVCO

POE, EDGAR ALLAN

Black Cat, The (short story)
    Black Cat, The (1941) U
    Tales of Terror (1962) AI

Case of M. Valdermar, The (short story)
    Tales of Terror (1962) AI

Fall of the House of Usher, The (short story)
    House of Usher, The (1960) AI

Gold Bug, The (short story)
    Jaws of Justice (1933) PRIN

Ligeia (short story)
    Tomb of Ligeia (1965) AI

Morella (short story)
    Tales of Terror (1962) AI

Murders in the Rue Morgue (short story)
    Murders in the Rue Morgue (1932) U
    Phantom of the Rue Morgue (1954) WB
    Murders in the Rue Morgue (1971) AI

Mystery of Marie Roget, The (short story)
    Mystery of Marie Roget, The (1942) U

Pit and the Pendulum, The (short story)
    Pit and the Pendulum, The (1961) AI

Premature Burial, The (short story)
    Crime of Dr. Crespi, The (1935) LIB/REP

Raven, The (poem)
    Raven, The (1935) U
    Raven, The (1953) AI

POLLOCK, CHANNING

Crowded Hour, The (play in collab. E. Selwyn)
    Crowded Hour, The (1925) PAR

Enemy, The (play)
    Enemy, The (1927) MGM

Fool, The (play)
    Fool, The (1925) F

Little Gray Lady (play)
    Little Gray Lady (1914) PAR

Sign on the Door, The (play)
    Sign on the Door, The (1921) FN
    Locked Door, The (1930) UA

Welcome Imposter, The (play)
    Midnight Intruder (1938) U

PONICSAN, DARYL

Cinderella Liberty (novel)
    Cinderella Liberty (1973) TCF

Last Detail, The (novel)
    Last Detail, The (1973) COL

PORTER, ELEANOR

Pollyanna (novel)
    Pollyanna (1920) UA
    Pollyanna (1960) BV

PORTER, KATHERINE ANNE

Ship of Fools (novel)
    Ship of Fools (1965) COL

PORTIS, CHARLES

True Grit (novel)
    True Grit (1969) PAR

PRESSBURGER, EMERIC

Killing a Mouse on Sunday (novel)
    Behold a Pale Horse (1964) COL

Monsieur Sans Gene (story)
    One Rainy Afternoon (1936) UA

PREVOST, ABBE

Manon Lescaut (novel)
    Manon Lescaut (1914) PFC
    When a Man Loves (1927) WB

PRIESTLY, J.B.

Old Dark House, The (novel)
    Old Dark House, The (1932) U

PROUTY, OLIVE HIGGINS

Now, Voyager (novel)
    Now, Voyager (1942) WB

Stella Dallas (novel)
    Stella Dallas (1925) UA
    Stella Dallas (1937) UA

PUSHKIN, ALEXANDER

Dubrovsky (novel)
    Eagle, The (1925) UA

PUZO, MARIO

Godfather, The (novel)
    Godfather, The (1972) PAR
    Godfather, Part II, The (1975) PAR

PYLE, HOWARD

Men of Iron (novel)
    Black Shield of Falworth, The (1954) UI

Q

QUEEN, ELLERY

Danger, Men Working (play in collab. Lowell
Brentano)
     Crime Nobody Saw, The (1937) PAR

R

RABE, DAVID

Streamers (play)
    Streamers (1983) UA

RAND, AYN

Fountainhead, The (novel)
    Fountainhead, The (1949) WB

Night of January 16th, The (play)
    Night of January 16th, The (1941) PAR

RAPHAEL, FREDERIC

Peter Ibbetson (play based on Du Maurier's novel)
    Forever (1921) PAR
    Peter Ibbetson (1935) PAR

RAPHAELSON, SAMSON

Accent on Youth (play)
    Accent on Youth (1935) PAR
    Mr. Music (1950) PAR
    But Not for Me (1959) PAR

Hilda Crane (play)
    Hilda Crane (1956) TCF

Jazz Singer, The (play)
    Jazz Singer, The (1927) WB
    Jazz Singer, The (1953) WB
    Jazz Singer, The (1980) ASF

La Couteriere de Luneville (play)
    Dressed to Thrill (1935) F

Letter to the Editor (story)
    Bannerline (1951) PAR

Perfect Marriage, The (play)
    Perfect Marriage, The (play)
    Perfect Marriage, The (1947) PAR

RATTIGAN, TERENCE

French Without Tears (play)
    French Without Tears (1940) PAR

Separate Tables (play)
    Separate Tables (1958) UA

Sleeping Prince, The (story)
    Prince and the Showgirl, The (1957) WB

RAWLINGS, MARJORIE KINNAN

Cross Creek (nonfiction)
    Cross Creek (1983) U

Sun Comes Up, The (novel)
    Sun Comes Up, The (1949) MGM

Yearling, The (novel)
    Yearling, The (1947) MGM

REED, BARRY

Verdict, The (novel)
    Verdict, The (1982) TCF

REED, MARK

Petticoat Fever (play)
    Petticoat Fever (1936) MGM

Yes, My Darling Daughter (play)
    Yes, My Darling Daughter (1939) WB

REMARQUE, ERICH MARIA

All Quiet on the Western Front (novel)
    All Quiet on the Western Front (1930) U

Arch of Triumph (novel)
    Arch of Triumph (1948) UA

Beyond (story)
    Other Love, The (1947) UA

Flotsam (novel)
    So Ends Our Night (1941) UA

Heaven Has No Favorites (novel)
    Bobby Deerfield (1977) COL

Road Back, The (novel)
    Road Back, The (1937) U

Three Comrades (novel)
    Three Comrades (1938) MGM

Time to Love and a Time to Die, A (novel)
    Time to Love and a Time to Die, A (1958) UI

REEVES, THEODORE

Glory Hole, The (story)
    Dangerous Waters (1936) U

Harbor, The (play)
    Society Doctor (1935) MGM

REYNOLDS, QUENTIN

West Side Miracle (novel)
    Secrets of a Nurse (1938) U

RICE, CRAIG

Home Sweet Homicide (novel)
    Home Sweet Homicide (1946) TCF

Lucky Stiff, The (novel)
    Lucky Stiff, The (1949) UA

Whipped, The (novel)
    Underworld Story, The (1950) UA

RICE, ELMER

Counsellor-at-Law (play)
    Counsellor-at-Law (1933) U

Doubling for Romeo (short story)
    Doubling for Romeo (1921) G

Dream Girl (play)
    Dream Girl (1948) PAR

On Trial (play)
    On Trial (1928) WB
    On Trial (1939) WB

See Naples and Die (play)
    Oh! Sailor, Behave! (1931) WB

Street Scene (play)
    Street Scene (1931) G

RICHMAN, ARTHUR

Ambush (play)
    Reckless Hour, The (1931) FN

Awful Truth, The (play)
    Awful Truth, The (1925) PDC
    Awful Truth, The (1937) COL
    Let's Do It Again (1953) COL

178

Not So Long Ago (play)
    Not So Long Ago (1925) PAR

RICHTER, CONRAD

Light in the Forest, The (novel)
    Light in the Forest, The (1958) BV

Sea of Grass, The (novel)
    Sea of Grass, The (1947) MGM

Tracey Cromwell (novel)
    One Desire (1955) UI

RIGGS, LYNN

Green Grow the Lilacs (play)
    Oklahoma! (1955) MTC

RILEY, JAMES WHITCOMB

Girl I Loved, The (poem)
    Girl I Loved, The (1923) UA

Old Swimmin' Hole, The (poem)
    Old Swimmin' Hole, The (1921) FN
    Old Swimmin' Hole, The (1940) MON

RILEY, LAWRENCE

Personal Appearance (play)
    Go West, Young Man (1936) PAR

RINEHART, MARY ROBERTS

Bab (story)
    Bab's Burglar (1917) PAR

Bat, The (play)
    Bat, The (1926) UA
    Bat Whispers, The (1931) UA
    Bat, The (1959) AA

179

Girl Who Was the Life of the Party (story)
     Girls Men Forget (1924) PRIN

Her Majesty the Queen (novel)
     Her Love Story (1924) PAR

K (novel)
     K - the Unknown (1924) U

Long Live the King (novel)
     Long Live the King (1923) M

Lost Ecstasy (novel)
     I Take This Woman (1931) PAR

Miss Pinkerton (story)
     Miss Pinkerton (1932) FN
     Nurse's Secret, The (1941) WB

Mr. Cohen Takes a Walk (short story)
     Mr. Cohen Takes a Walk (1936) WB

State vs. Elinor Norton (story)
     Elinor Norton (1935) F

Tumble In (play in collab. A. Hopwood)
     Seven Days (1925) UDC

23 1/2 Hours' Leave (novel)
     23 1/2 Hours' Leave (1919) PAR
     23 1/2 Hours' Leave (1937) GN

RIPLEY, CLEMENTS

Dust and Sun (novel)
     Devil With Women, A (1930) F

Gold Is Where You Find It (story)
     Gold Is Where You Find It (1938) WB

RITCHIE, JACK

Green Heart, The (short story)
     New Leaf, A (1971) PAR

ROBBINS, HAROLD

Betsy, The (novel)
        Betsy, The (1978) AA

Carpetbaggers, The (novel)
        Carpetbaggers, The (1964) PAR

Lonely Lady, The (novel)
        Lonely Lady, The (1983) U

Never Love a Stranger (novel)
        Never Love a Stranger (1958) AA

Stiletto (novel)
        Stiletto (1969) AVCO

Stone for Danny Fisher, A (novel)
        King Creole (1958) PAR

Where Love Has Gone (novel)
        Where Love Has Gone (1964) PAR

ROBERTS, KENNETH

Captain Caution (novel)
        Captain Caution (1940) UA

Lydia Bailey (novel)
        Lydia Bailey (1952) TCF

Northwest Passage (novel)
        Northwest Passage (1940) MGM

ROBESON, KENNETH

Doc Savage the Man of Bronze (novel)
        Doc Savage the Man of Bronze (1975) WB

ROHMER, SAX

Daughter of Fu Manchu (novel)
        Daughter of the Dragon (1931) PAR

Mask of Fu Manchu, The (novel)

Mask of Fu Manchu, The (1932) PAR

Mysterious Dr. Fu Manchu, The (novel)
    Mysterious Dr. Fu Manchu, The (1929) PAR

ROONEY, FRANK

Cyclists' Raid, The (short story)
    Wild One, The (1954) COL

ROOT, LYNN

Hello, Hollywood (story in collab. Frank Fenton)
    Keep Smiling (1938) TCF

Milky Way, The (play in collab. H. Clork)
    Milky Way, The (1936) PAR

Shanghai Deadline (story in collab. Frank Fenton)
    International Settlement (1938) F

Southerner (story in collab. Bess Meredyth)
    Prodigal, The (1931) MGM

ROPES, BRADFORD

Forty-Second Street (novel)
    Forty-Second Street (1933) WB

Go Into Your Dance (novel)
    Go Into Your Dance (1935) WB

Stage Mother (novel)
    Stage Mother (1933) MGM

ROSTAND, EDMOND

Cyrano de Bergerac (play)
    Cyrano de Bergerac (1950) UA

ROSTAND, MAURICE

Man I Killed, The (play)

182

Man I Killed, The (ret. Broken Lullaby) (1932)
PAR

ROSTEN, LEO

Captain Newman, M.D. (novel)
    Captain Newman, M.D. (1964) U

Sleep, My Love (novel)
    Sleep, My Love (1948) UA

ROTH, JOSEPH

Job (novel)
    Sins of Man (1936) TCF

ROTH, PHILIP

Goodbye, Columbus (novel)
    Goodbye, Columbus (1969) PAR

Portnoy's Complaint (novel)
    Portnoy's Complaint (1972) WB

ROUVEROL, AURANIA

Skidding (play)
    Family Affair, A (1937) MGM

ROYLE, EDWIN MILTON

Squaw Man, The (play)
    Squaw Man, The (1913) PAR
    Squaw Man, The (1918) PAR
    Squaw Man, The (1931) MGM

RUNYON, DAMON

Big Mitten (short story)
    No Ransom (1935) LIB

Bloodhounds of Broadway (short story)

Bloodhounds of Broadway (1952) TCF

Butch Minds the Baby (short story)
    Butch Minds the Baby (1942) U

Call on the President, A (short story)
    Joe and Ethel Turp Call on the President
    (1939) MGM

Gentlemen, the King (short story)
    Professional Soldier (1935) TCF

Guys and Dolls (short story)
    Very Honorable Guy, A (1934) FN
    Guys and Dolls (1955) MGM

Hold 'Em, Yale (short story)
    Hold 'Em, Yale (1935) PAR

Lemon Drop Kid, The (short story)
    Lemon Drop Kid, The (1934) PAR
    Lemon Drop Kid, The (1951) PAR

Little Miss Marker (short story)
    Little Miss Marker (1934) PAR
    Sorrowful Jones (1949) PAR
    Little Miss Marker (1980) U

Little Pinks (short story)
    Big Street, The (1942) RKO

Madame La Gimp (short story)
    Lady for a Day (1933) COL
    Pocketful of Miracles (1961) UA

Million Dollar Ransom (short story)
    Million Dollar Ransom (1934) U

Money From Home (short story)
    Money From Home (1954) PAR

Old Doll's House (short story)
    Midnight Alibi (1934) FN

Princess O'Hara (short story)
    Princess O'Hara (1935) U

Slight Case of Murder, A (play in collab. H. Lindsay)
    Slight Case of Murder, A (1938) WB
    Stop, You're Killing Me (1952) WB

Three Wise Guys, The (short story)
    Three Wise Guys, The (1936) MGM

Tight Shoes (short story)
    Tight Shoes (1941) U

RUSSELL, JOHN

Firewalker, The (story)
    Girl of the Port (1930) RKO

Lost God, The (story)
    Sea God, The (1930) PAR

Pagan, The (story)
    Pagan, The (1929) MGM

Passion Vine, The (story)
    Where the Pavement Ends (1923) M

Red Mark, The (story)
    Red Mark, The (1928) PAT

RYAN, CORNELIUS

Longest Day, The (nonfiction)
    Longest Day, The (1962) TCF

185

SABATINI, RAFAEL

Bardelys the Magnificent (novel)
    Bardelys the Magnificent (1926) MGM

Black Swan, The(novel)
    Black Swan, The (1942) TCF

Captain Blood (novel)
    Captain Blood (1924) VIT
    Captain Blood (1935) WB

Captain Blood Returns (novel)
    Captain Pirate (1952) COL

Fortunes of Captain Blood (novel)
    Fortunes of Captain Blood (1950) COL

Scaramouche (novel)
    Scaramouche (1923) ME
    Scaramouche (1952) MGM

Sea Hawk, The (novel)
    Sea Hawk, The (1924) FN
    Sea Hawk, The (1940) WB

SACKLER, HOWARD

Great White Hope, The (play)
    Great White Hope, The (1970) TCF

SAGAN, FRANCOISE

Aimez-vous Brahms? (novel)
    Goodbye Again (1961) UA

Bonjour Tristesse (novel)
    Bonjour Tristesse (1958) COL

Certain Smile, A (novel)
    Certain Smile, A (1958) TCF

SALE, RICHARD

Not Too Narrow, Not Too Deep (novel)
    Strange Cargo (1940) MGM

Oscar, The (novel)
    Oscar, The (1966) EMB

Rendezvous With Annie (story in collab. Mary Loos)
    Rendezvous With Annie (1946) REP

White Buffalo, The (novel)
    White Buffalo, The (1977) UA

SALINGER, J.D.

Uncle Wiggily in Connecticut (short story)
    My Foolish Heart (1950) RKO

SALTEN, FELIX

Bambi (novel)
    Bambi (anim. 1942) RKO

Hound of Florence, The (novel)
    Shaggy Dog, The (1959) BV

SANDERS, LAWRENCE

187

Anderson Tapes, The (novel)
    Anderson Tapes, The (1971) COL

SARDOU, VICTORIEN

Cyprienne (play)
    Don't Tell the Wife (1927) WB

Diplomacy (play)
    Diplomacy (1926) PAR

Divorcons (play)
    Let's Get a Divorce (1918) PAR

Fedora (play)
    Fedora (1918) PAR
    Woman From Moscow, The (1928) PAR

Ferreol (play)
    Night of Mystery, A (1928) PAR

Madame Sans-Gene (play in collab. Emile Moreau)
    Madame Sans-Gene (1925) PAR

SAROYAN, WILLIAM

Human Comedy, The (novel)
    Human Comedy, The (1943) MGM

Time of Your Life, The (play)
    Time of Your Life, The (1948) UA

SAUNDERS, JOHN MONK

Air Devils (story)
    Devil Dogs of the Air (1935) WB

Dockwalloper, The (story)
    Docks of New York (1928) PAR

Judas Tree, The (story)
    I Found Stella Parish (1935) FN

Maker of Gestures, A (novel)

Too Many Kisses (1925) PAR

Shock Punch, The (play)
    Shock Punch, The (1925) PAR

Single Lady (novel)
    Last Flight, The (1931) FN

SAVOIR, ALFRED

Banco (play)
    Lost - A Wife (1925) PAR

Bluebeard's Eighth Wife (play)
    Bluebeard's Eighth Wife (1923) PAR
    Bluebeard's Eighth Wife (1938) PAR

Grand Duchess and the Waiter, The (play)
    Grand Duchess and the Waiter, The (1926) PAR
    Here Is My Heart (1934) PAR

Supper of the Gaiety (play)
    His Tiger Lady (1928) PAR

SAYERS, DOROTHY L.

Busman's Honeymoon (novel, play)
    Haunted Honeymoon (1940) MGM

SCHAEFER, JACK

Advance to the Rear (novel)
    Advance to the Rear (1964) MGM

Monte Walsh (novel)
    Monte Walsh (1970) CC

Shane (novel)
    Shane (1953) PAR

SCHARY, DORE

Loves of a Sailor (story in collab. Lewis Foster)
    Let's Talk It Over (1934) U

Sunrise at Campobello (play)
    Sunrise at Campobello (1960) WB

SCHNITZLER, ARTHUR

Daybreak (novel)
    Daybreak (1931) MGM

SCHULBERG, BUDD

Harder They Fall, The (novel)
    Harder They Fall, The (1956) COL

Your Arkansas Traveler (novel)
    Face in the Crowd, A (1957) WB

SCOTT, LEROY

Counterfeit (novel)
    Flirting With Love (1924) FN

Little Angel (novel)
    Lady of Chance (1929) MGM

Mother, The (story)
    Poverty of Riches (1921) G

Mother O'Day (novel)
    City That Never Sleeps, The (1924) PAR

Partners of the Night (novel)
    Partners of the Night (1920) G

Thirteen Washington Square (play)
    Thirteen Washington Square (1928) U

SCOTT, SIR WALTER

Ivanhoe (novel)
    Ivanhoe (1952) MGM

Quentin Durward (novel)
     Quentin Durward (1955) MGM

Talisman, The (novel)
     Richard the Lion-Hearted (1923) APD
     King Richard and the Crusades (1954) WB

SEGAL, ERICH

Love Story (novel)
     Love Story (1970) PAR

Man, Woman and Child (novel)
     Man, Woman and Child (1983) PAR

Oliver's Story (novel)
     Oliver's Story (1978) PAR

SELWYN, EDGAR

Arab, The (play)
     Arab, The (1924) MG

Crowded Hour, The (play in collab. C. Pollock)
     Crowded Hour, The (1925) PAR

Dancing Mothers (play in collab. Edmund Goulding)
     Dancing Mothers (1926) PAR

Divorce, The (play)
     Primitive Lover, The (1922) FN

Mirage, The (play)
     Possessed (1931) MGM

Pierre of the Plains (play)
     Heart of the Wilds (1918) ART
     Over the Border (1922) PAR
     Pierre of the Plains (1942) MGM

SERVICE, ROBERT W.

Poisoned Paradise (novel)
     Poisoned Paradise (1924) PRE

Roughneck, The (poem)
    Roughneck, The (1924) F

Shooting of Dan McGrew, The (poem)
    Shooting of Dan McGrew, The (1924) MG

Trail of '98, The (novel)
    Trail of '98, The (1928) MGM

SEWELL, ANNA

Black Beauty (novel)
    Black Beauty (1921) VIT
    Black Beauty (1933) MON
    Black Beauty (1946) TCF

SHAFFER, PETER

Equus (play)
    Equus (1977) UA

SHAGAN, STEVE

Formula, The (novel)
    Formula, The (1980) MGM/UA

SHAKESPEARE, WILLIAM

As You Like It (play)
    As You Like It (1912)

Cymbeline (play)
    Cymbeline (1913)

Julius Caesar (play)
    Julius Caesar (1952) AVON
    Julius Caesar (1953) MGM

King Lear (play)
    King Lear (1916) THAN

Macbeth (play)
    Macbeth (1916) REI

Macbeth (1950) COL

Merchant of Venice, The (play)
    Merchant of Venice, The (1912)
    Merchant of Venice, The (1914)

Midsummer Night's Dream, A (play)
    Midsummer Night's Dream, A (1935) WB

Othello (play)
    Othello (1955) UA
    Catch My Soul (1974) CINERAMA

Richard III (play)
    Richard III (1913)

Romeo and Juliet (play)
    Romeo and Juliet (1911) THAN
    Romeo and Juliet (1916) M
    Romeo and Juliet (1936) MGM

Taming of the Shrew, The (play)
    Taming of the Shrew, The (1908) VIT
    Taming of the Shrew, The (1929) UA
    Taming of the Shrew, The (1967) COL

SHAW, GEORGE BERNARD

Androcles and the Lion (play)
    Androcles and the Lion (1953) RKO

Devil's Disciple, The (play)
    Devil's Disciple, The (1959) UA

Pygmalion (play)
    My Fair Lady (1964) WB

Saint Joan (play)
    Saint Joan (1957) UA

SHAW, IRWIN

Education of the Heart (story)
    Easy Living (1949) RKO

Gentle People, The (play)

Out of the Fog (1941) WB

Night Call (story in collab. David Shaw)
    Take One False Step (1949) U

Then We Were Three (short story)
    Three (1969) UA

Tip on a Dead Jockey (short story)
    Tip on a Dead Jockey (1957) MGM

Two Weeks in Another Town (novel)
    Two Weeks in Another Town (1962) MGM

Year to Learn the Language, A (short story)
    In the French Style (1963) COL

Young Lions, The (novel)
    Young Lions, The (1958) TCF

SHELDON, CHARLES M.

In His Steps (novel)
    In His Steps (1936) GN

SHELDON, EDWARD

Dishonored Lady (play in collab. Margaret Barnes)
    Dishonored Lady (1947) UA

Egypt (play)
    Call of Her People, The (1917) M

Lulu Belle (play in collab. C. MacArthur)
    Lulu Belle (1948) COL

Princess Zim Zim (play)
    Coney Island Princess (1916) PAR

Romance (play)
    Romance (1920) UA
    Romance (1930) MGM

Salvation Nell (play)
    Salvation Nell (1915) WO
    Salvation Nell (1921) FN

Salvation Nell (1931) TIF

Song of Songs, The (play)
      Song of Songs, The (1918) ART
      Lily of the Dust (1924) PAR
      Song of Songs, The (1933) PAR

SHELDON, SIDNEY

Bloodline (novel)
      Bloodline (1979) PAR

Other Side of Midnight, The (novel)
      Other Side of Midnight, The (1977) TCF

SHELLEY, MARY

Frankenstein (novel)
      Frankenstein (1931) U

SHEPHERD, JEAN

In God We Trust, All Others Pay Cash (nonfiction)
      Christmas Story, A (1983) MGM/UA

SHERRIFF, R.C.

Journey's End (play)
      Journey's End (1930) TIF

SHERWOOD, ROBERT E.

Abe Lincoln in Illinois (play)
      Abe Lincoln in Illinois (1940) RKO

Idiot's Delight (play)
      Idiot's Delight (1939) MGM

Petrified Forest, The (play)
      Petrified Forest, The (1936) WB
      Escape in the Desert (1945) WB

Queen's Husband, The (play)
      Royal Bed, The (1931) RKO

Reunion in Vienna (play)
    Reunion in Vienna (1933) MGM

Road to Rome (play)
    Jupiter's Darling (1955) MGM

This Is New York (play)
    Two Kinds of Women (1932) PAR

Waterloo Bridge (play)
    Waterloo Bridge (1931) U
    Waterloo Bridge (1940) MGM
    Gaby (1956) MGM

SHIPMAN, SAMUEL

Cheaper to Marry (play)
    Cheaper to Marry (1925) MG

East Is West (play in collab. John B. Hymer)
    East Is West (1930) U

Fast Life (play in collab. John B. Hymer)
    Fast Life (1929) FN

Friendly Enemies (play in collab. Aaron Hoffman)
    Friendly Enemies (1925) PDC
    Friendly Enemies (1942) UA

Lawful Larceny (play)
    Lawful Larceny (1923) PAR
    Lawful Larceny (1930) RKO

Manhattan Parade (play)
    Manhattan Parade (1932) WB

Pay-Off, The (play in collab. John B. Hymer)
    Pay-Off, The (1930) RKO

Scarlet Pages (play in collab. John B. Hymer)
    Scarlet Pages (1930) FN

Woman in Room 13, The (play in collab. with others)
    Woman in Room 13, The (1920) G
    Woman in Room 13, The (1932) F

SHIRK, ADAM HULL

House of Mystery, The (play)
    House of Mystery, The (1934) MON

SHORT, LUKE

Blood on the Moon (novel)
    Blood on the Moon (1948) RKO

Dead Freight for Plute (novel)
    Albuquerque (1948) PAR

High Vermillion (story)
    Silver City (1951) PAR

Silver Rock (novel)
    Hell's Outpost (1955) REP

SHULMAN, IRVING

Amboy Dukes, The (novel)
    City Across the River (1949) U

SHUTE, NEVILLE

No Highway (novel)
    No Highway in the Sky (1951) TCF

On the Beach (novel)
    On the Beach (19459) UA

Pied Piper, The (novel)
    Pied Piper, The (1942) TCF

SIENKIEWICZ, HENRYK

Quo Vadis? (novel)
    Quo Vadis (1951) MGM

SIMENON, GEORGES

Battle of Nerves, A (novel)
    Man on the Eiffel Tower, The (1949) RKO

Bottom of the Bottle, The (novel)
    Bottom of the Bottle, The (1956) TCF

Matter of Life and Death, A (novel)
    Life in the Balance, A (1955) TCF

SIMON, NEIL

Barefoot in the Park (play)
    Barefoot in the Park (1967) PAR

California Suite (play)
    California Suite (1978) COL

Come Blow Your Horn (play)
    Come Blow Your Horn (1963) PAR

Gingerbread Lady, The (play)
    Only When I Laugh (1981) COL

I Ought to Be in Pictures (play)
    I Ought to Be in Pictures (1982) TCF

Last of the Red Hot Lovers (play)
    Last of the Red Hot Lovers (1972) PAR

Odd Couple, The (play)
    Odd Couple, The (1968) PAR

Plaza Suite (play)
    Plaza Suite (1971) PAR

Prisoner of Second Avenue, The (play)
    Prisoner of Second Avenue, The (1975) WB

Star Spangled Girl (play)
    Star Spangled Girl (1971) PAR

Sunshine Boys, The (play)
    Sunshine Boys, The (1975) UA

Sweet Charity (play in collab. Cy Coleman, Dorothy
Fields)
    Sweet Charity (1969) U

SIMON, ROGER L.

Big Fix, The (novel)
    Big Fix, The (1978) U

SINCLAIR, UPTON

Gnome-Mobile, The (novel)
    Gnome-Mobile, The (1967) BV

Jungle, The (novel)
    Jungle, The (1914) ALL-STAR

Wet Parade, The (novel)
    Wet Parade, The (1932) MGM

SINGER, ISAAC BASHEVIS

Yentl, the Yeshiva Boy (story)
    Yentl (1983) MGM/UA

SIODMAK; CURT

Donovan's Brain (novel)
    Lady and the Monster, The (1944) REP
    Donovan's Brain (1953) UA

Friday the 13th (story in collab. Eric Taylor)
    Black Friday (1940) U

SKLAR, GEORGE

Merry Go Round (play in collab. Albert Maltz)
    Afraid to Talk (1932) U

SLADE, BERNARD

Romantic Comedy (play)
    Romantic Comedy (1983) MGM/UA

Same Time, Next Year (play)
    Same Time, Next Year (1978) U

Tribute (play)

Tribute (1981) TCF

SLAUGHTER, FRANK G.

Doctor's Wives (novel)
    Doctor's Wives (1971) COL

Sangaree (novel)
    Sangaree (1953) PAR

Warrior, The (novel)
    Naked in the Sun (1957) AA

SMITH, BETTY

Tree Grows in Brooklyn, A (novel)
    Tree Grows in Brooklyn, A (1944) TCF

SMITH, J. AUGUSTUS

Drums o' Voodoo (play)
    Drums o' Voodoo (1934) INS

SMITH, MARTIN CRUZ

Gorky Park (novel)
    Gorky Park (1983) ORION

SMITH, THORNE

Night Life of the Gods (novel)
    Night Life of the Gods (1935) U

Topper (novel)
    Topper (1937) MGM

Topper Takes a Trip (novel)
    Topper Takes a Trip (1938) UA

Turnabout (novel)
    Turnabout (1940) UA

SPARK, MURIEL

Prime of Miss Jean Brodie, The (novel)
    Prime of Miss Jean Brodie, The (1969) TCF

SPEWACK, BELLA AND SAMUEL

Boy Meets Girl (play)
    Boy Meets Girl (1938) WB

Clear All Wires (play)
    Clear All Wires (1933) MGM

Kiss Me, Kate (play)
    Kiss Me, Kate (1953) MGM

Solitaire Man, The (play)
    Solitaire Man, The (1933) MGM

SPILLANE, MICKEY

I, the Jury (novel)
    I, the Jury (1953) UA
    I, the Jury (1982) TCF

Long Wait, The (novel)
    Long Wait, The (1954) UA

SPYRI, JOHANNA

Heidi (novel)
    Heidi (1937) TCF
    Heidi's Song (1982) P

STALLINGS, LAURENCE

Rainbow (play in collab. O. Hammerstein II)
    Song of the West (1930) WB

What Price Glory (play in collab. M. Anderson)
    What Price Glory (1926) F
    What Price Glory (1952) TCF

STEINBECK, JOHN

Cannery Row (novel)
    Cannery Row (1982) MGM/UA

East of Eden (novel)
    East of Eden (1955) WB

Grapes of Wrath, The (novel)
    Grapes of Wrath, The (1940) TCF

Moon Is Down, The (novel, play)
    Moon Is Down, The (1943) TCF

Of Mice and Men (novel, play)
    Of Mice and Men (1939) UA

Red Pony, The (novel)
    Red Pony, The (1949) REP

Sweet Thursday (novel)
    Cannery Row (1982) MGM/UA

Tortilla Flat (novel)
    Tortilla Flat (1942) MGM

Wayward Bus, The (novel)
    Wayward Bus, The (1957) TCF

STEPHENSON, CARL

Leinengen vs. the Ants (short story)
    Naked Jungle, The (1964) PAR

STERN, PHILIP VAN DOREN

Greatest Gift, The (short story)
    It's a Wonderful Life (1946) RKO

STEVENSON, ROBERT LOUIS

Black Arrow, The (novel)
    Black Arrow, The (1948) COL

Body Snatcher, The (short story)

Body Snatcher, The (1945) RKO

Dr. Jekyll and Mr. Hyde (short story)
     Dr. Jekyll and Mr. Hyde (1920) PAR
     Dr. Jekyll and Mr. Hyde (1932) PAR
     Dr. Jekyll and Mr. Hyde (1942) MGM
     House of Fright (1961) AI

Ebb Tide (short story)
     Ebb Tide (1922) PAR
     Ebb Tide (1937) PAR
     Adventure Island (1947) PAR

Kidnapped (novel)
     Kidnapped (1938) TCF
     Kidnapped (1960) BV

Master of Ballantrae, The (novel)
     Master of Ballantrae, The (1953) WB

Pavilion on the Links, The (short story)
     White Circle, The (1920) PAR

Silverado Squatters (story)
     Adventures in Silverado (1948) COL

Sire de Maletroit's Door, The (short story)
     Strange Door, The (1951) UI

Suicide Club, The (story)
     Trouble for Two (1936) MGM

Treasure Island (novel)
     Treasure Island (1918) F
     Treasure Island (1920) PAR
     Treasure Island (1934) MGM
     Treasure Island (1950) RKO

Treasure of Franchard, The (story)
     Treasure of Lost Canyon, The (1952) U

STEWART, FRED M.

Six Weeks (novel)
     Six Weeks (1982) U

STOKER, BRAM

Dracula (novel)
    Dracula (1931) U
    Dracula (1979) U
    Horror of Dracula (1958) U

Jewel of Seven Stars, The (novel)
    Awakening, The (1980) ORION

STONE, IRVING

Agony and the Ecstasy, The (novel)
    Agony and the Ecstasy, The (1965) TCF

False Witness (novel)
    Arkansas Judge (1941) REP

Lust for Life (novel)
    Lust for Life (1956) MGM

President's Lady, The (novel)
    President's Lady, The (1953) TCF

STONG, PHIL

Career (novel)
    Career (1939) RKO

Farmer in the Dell, The (novel)
    Farmer in the Dell, The (1936) RKO

State Fair (novel)
    State Fair (1933) F
    State Fair (1945) TCF
    State Fair (1962) TCF

Stranger's Return, The (novel)
    Stranger's Return, The (1933) MGM

STOUT, REX

Fer de Lance (novel)
    Meet Nero Wolfe (1936) COL

STOWE, HARRIET BEECHER

My Wife and I (novel)
    My Wife and I (1925) WB

Uncle Tom's Cabin (novel)
    Uncle Tom's Cabin (1915) PAR
    Uncle Tom's Cabin (1927) U

STRACHEY, LYTTON

Eminent Victorians (biography)
    White Angel, The (1936) WB

STRATTON-PORTER, MRS. GENE

Freckles (novel)
    Freckles (1935) RKO

Girl of the Limberlost, A (novel)
    Girl of the Limberlost, A (1934) MON

Harvester, The (novel)
    Harvester, The (1927) FBO
    Harvester, The (1936) REP

Her Father's Daughter (story)
    Her First Romance (1940) MON

Keeper of the Bees, The (novel)
    Keeper of the Bees, The (1925) FBO
    Keeper of the Bees, The (1935) MON

Laddie (novel)
    Laddie (1935) RKO

STRAUB, PETER

Ghost Story (novel)
    Ghost Story (1981) U

STREET, EDWARD

Father of the Bride   (novel)
      Father of the Bride (1950) MGM

STRONG, AUSTIN

Seventh Heaven (play)
      Seventh Heaven (1927) F
      Seventh Heaven (1937) TCF

Three Wise Fools (play)
      Three Wise Fools (1946) MGM

STURGES, PRESTON

Child of Manhattan (play)
      Child of Manhattan (1933) COL

Strictly Dishonorable (play)
      Strictly Dishonorable (1931) U
      Strictly Dishonorable (1951) MGM

STYRON, WILLIAM

Sophie's Choice (novel)
      Sophie's Choice (1982) U

SUDERMANN, HERMANN

Song of Songs, The (novel; play by E. Sheldon)
      Lily of the Dust (1924) PAR
      Song of Songs (1933) PAR

Trip to Tilsit, A (story)
      Sunrise (1927) F

Undying Past, The (novel)
      Flesh and the Devil (1927) MGM

Wife of Stephen Trumhold (story)
      Wonder of Women, The (1929) MGM

SULLIVAN, ED

Fashions for Sale (story)
    Ma, He's Making Eyes at Me (1940) U

SUMNER, CID RICKETTS

Quality (novel)
    Pinky (1949) TCF

Tammy and the Bachelor (novel)
    Tammy and the Bachelor (1957) U

SUSANN, JACQUELINE

Love Machine, The (novel)
    Love Machine, The (1971) COL

Valley of the Dolls (novel)
    Valley of the Dolls (1967) TCF

SUTRO, ALFRED

Great Well, The (novel)
    Neglected Woman (1924) FBO

Laughing Lady, The (play)
    Society Scandal, A (1924) PAR
    Laughing Lady, The (1930) PAR

SWIFT, JONATHAN

Gulliver's Travels (novel)
    Gulliver's Travels (anim. 1939)
    Three Worlds of Gulliver, The (1960) COL

SYRETT, NETTA

Portrait of a Rebel (novel)
    Woman Rebels, A (1936) RKO

T

TARKINGTON, BOOTH

Alice Adams (novel)
    Alice Adams (1935) RKO

Cameo Kirby (play in collab. Harry L. Wilson)
    Cameo Kirby (1923) F
    Cameo Kirby (1930) F

Clarence (play)
    Clarence (1922) PAR
    Clarence (1937) PAR

Conquest of Canaan, The (novel)
    Conquest of Canaan, The (1916) FRO
    Conquest of Canaan, The (1921) PAR

Flirt, The (story)
    Bad Sister (1931) U

Gentle Julia (novel)
    Gentle Julia (1936) TCF

Gentleman From Louisiana, The (novel)
    Gentleman From Louisiana, The (1915) PALLAS

Geraldine (story)
    Geraldine (1928) PAT

Magnificent Ambersons, The (novel)
    Pampered Youth (1925) VIT
    Magnificent Ambersons, The (1942) RKO

Magnolia (play)
    Fighting Coward, The (1924) PAR
    River of Romance (1929) PAR
    Mississippi (1935) PAR

Man From Home, The (play in collab. Harry L.
Wilson)
    Man From Home, The (1922) PAR

Man Who Found Himself, The (story)
    Man Who Found Himself, The (1925) PAR

Misunderstood (story)
    Boy of Mine (1923) FN

Monsieur Beaucaire (novel)
    Monsieur Beaucaire (1924) PAR
    Monsieur Beaucaire (1946) PAR

Old Fathers and Young Sons (story)
    Father's Son (1931) FN
    Old Fathers and Young Sons (1941) WB

Penrod (short stories)
    Penrod (1922) FN

Penrod and Sam (novel)
    Penrod and Sam (1923) FN
    Penrod and Sam (1931) FN
    Penrod and Sam (1937) WB

Pied Piper Malone (short story)
    Pied Piper Malone (1924) PAR

Plutocrat, The (novel)
    Business and Pleasure (1932) F

Presenting Lily Mars (novel)
    Presenting Lily Mars (1943) MGM

Seventeen (novel)
    Seventeen (1940) PAR

TAYLOR, KRESSMAN

Address Unknown (short story)
    Address Unknown (1944) COL

TENNYSON, ALFRED, LORD

Beggar Maid, The (poem)
    Beggar Maid, The (1921) TRIART

TERHUNE, ALBERT PAYSON

Driftwood (story)
    Daring Love (1924) TRUART

Grand Larceny (short story)
    Grand Larceny (1922) G

His Dog (novel)
    His Dog (1927) PAT
    Lad: A Dog (1963) WB

Hunch, The (story)
    Knockout Reilly (1927) PAR

Lotus Eater, The (short story)
    Lotus Eater, The (1921) FN

Night of the Dub, The (short story)
    Night of the Dub, The (1920) PAR

Treve (novel)
    Mighty Treve, The (1937) U

THACKERAY, WILLIAM MAKEPEACE

Vanity Fair (novel)
    Vanity Fair (1915) EDK
    Vanity Fair (1923) G
    Becky Sharp (1935) RKO

THAYER, ERNEST LAWRENCE

Casey at the Bat (poem)

Casey at the Bat (1916) FAT
Casey at the Bat (1927) PAR

THAYER, TIFFANY

Call Her Savage (novel)
    Call Her Savage (1932) F

Illustrious Corpse, The (novel)
    Strangers of the Evening (1932) TIF

King of Gamblers (story)
    King of Gamblers (1937) PAR

One Woman (story)
    Chicago Deadline (1949) PAR

Thirteen Women (novel)
    Thirteen Women (1932) RKO

THOMAS, A.E.

Come Out of the Kitchen (play in collab. Alice
Miller)
    Come Out of the Kitchen (1919) PAR

French Doll, The (play)
    French Doll, The (1923) M

Girl Habit, The (play in collab. Clayton Hamilton)
    Girl Habit, The (1931) PAR

Just Suppose (play)
    Just Suppose (1926) FN

No More Ladies (play)
    No More Ladies (1935) MGM

Squadrons (play in collab. E.W. Spring)
    Body and Soul (1931) F

Thirty Days (play in collab. Clayton Hamilton)
    Thirty Days (1922) PAR

World's Champion, The (play in collab. T. Louden)
    World's Champion, The (1922) PAR

THOMAS, AUGUSTUS

Arizona (play)
    Arizona (1918) ART
    Men Are Like That (1931) COL

Copperhead, The (play)
    Copperhead, The (1920) PAR

In Mizzoura (play)
    In Mizzoura (1919) PAR

Witching Hour, The (play)
    Witching Hour, The (1916) FRO
    Witching Hour, The (1934) PAR

THOMAS, BRANDON

Charley's Aunt (play)
    Charley's Aunt (1925) PDC
    Charley's Aunt (1930) COL
    Charley's Aunt (1941) TCF
    Where's Charlie? (1952) WB

THOMPSON, DENMAN

Old Homestead, The (play)
    Old Homestead, The (1915) PAR
    Old Homestead, The (1922) PAR
    Old Homestead, The (1935) LIB
    Old Homestead, The (1942) REP

THOMPSON, ERNEST

On Golden Pond (play)
    On Golden Pond (1981) U

THURBER, JAMES

Male Animal, The (play in collab. Elliot Nugent)
    Male Animal, The (1942) WB
    She's Working Her Way Through College (1952)

PAR

My Life and Times (nonfiction)
    Rise and Shine (1941) TCF

Secret Life of Walter Mitty, The (short story)
    Secret Life of Walter Mitty, The (1947) RKO

TOLKIEN, J.R.R.

Lord of the Rings, The (novel)
    Lord of the Rings, The (anim. 1978) UA

TOLSTOY, LEO

Anna Karenina (novel)
    Love (1927) MGM
    Anna Karenina (1935) MGM

Cossacks, The (novel)
    Cossacks, The (1923) MGM

Living Corpse, The (play)
    Redemption (1930) MGM

Resurrection (novel)
    Resurrection (1918) PAR
    Resurrection (1927) UA
    Resurrection (1930) U
    We Live Again (1934) UA

War and Peace (novel)
    War and Peace (1956) PAR

TOWNSEND, EDWARD W.

Chimmie Fadden Out West (short story)
    Chimmie Fadden Out West (1915) PAR

TRAIL, ARMITAGE

Scarface (novel)
    Scarface (1931) UA
    Scarface (1983) U

Thirteenth Guest, The (novel)
    Mystery of the 13th Guest, The (1943) MON

TRAVEN, B.

Treasure of Sierra Madre, The (novel)
    Treasure of Sierra Madre, The (1948) WB

TRUMBO, DALTON

Johnny Got His Gun (novel)
    Johnny Got His Gun (1971) CINEMATION

Lady Takes a Chance (story)
    Half a Sinner (1940) U

Remarkable Andrew, The (novel)
    Remarkable Andrew, The (1942) PAR

TRYON, TOM

Other, The (novel)
    Other, The (1972) TCF

TUCHMAN, BARBARA

Guns of August, The (nonfiction)
    Guns of August, The (doc. 1964) U

TULLY, RICHARD WALTON

Bird of Paradise, The (play)
    Bird of Paradise (1932) RKO
    Bird of Paradise (1951) TCF

Rose of the Rancho (play in collab. D. Belasco)
    Rose of the Rancho (1936) PAR

TWAIN, MARK

Adventures of Huckleberry Finn (novel)

Huckleberry Finn (1920) PAR
Huckleberry Finn (1931) PAR
Adventures of Huckleberry Finn (1939) MGM
Adventures of Huckleberry Finn (1960) MGM
Huckleberry Finn (1974) UA

Adventures of Tom Sawyer (novel)
    Tom Sawyer (1917) PAR
    Tom Sawyer (1930) PAR
    Adventures of Tom Sawyer (1938) UA
    Tom Sawyer (1973) UA

Celebrated Jumping Frog of Calaveras County, The
(short story)
    Best Man Wins (1948) COL

Connecticut Yankee in King Arthur's Court, A
(novel)
    Connecticut Yankee in King Arthur's Court, A
    (1921) F
    Connecticut Yankee, A (1931) F
    Connecticut Yankee in King Arthur's Court, A
    (1949) PAR

Further Adventures of Tom Sawyer (novel)
    Huck and Tom (1918) PAR

Million Pound Bank Note, The (short story)
    Man With a Million (1954) UA

Prince and the Pauper, The (novel)
    Prince and the Pauper, The (1915) PAR
    Prince and the Pauper, The (1937) WB
    Crossed Swords (1978) WB

Tom Sawyer, Detective (novel)
    Tom Sawyer, Detective (1938) PAR

Tragedy of Pudd'nhead Wilson, The (novel)
    Pudd'n Head Wilson (1916) PAR

U

UPDIKE, JOHN

Too Far to Go (stories)
    Too Far to Go (1982) ZOETROPE

URIS, LEON

Battle Cry (novel)
    Battle Cry (1955) WB

Exodus (novel)
    Exodus (1960) UA

Topaz (novel)
    Topaz (1969) U

USTINOV, PETER

Romanoff and Juliet (play)
    Romanoff and Juliet (1961) UI

216

V

VALDEZ, LUIS

Zoot Suit (play)
    Zoot Suit (1982) U

VAN DINE, S.S.

Benson Murder Case, The (novel)
    Benson Murder Case, The (1930) PAR

Bishop Murder Case, The (novel)
    Bishop Murder Case, The (1930) MGM

Canary Murder Case, The (novel)
    Canary Murder Case, The (1929) PAR

Casino Murder Case, The (novel)
    Casino Murder Case, The (1935) MGM

Dragon Murder Case, The (novel)
    Dragon Murder Case, The (1934) FN

Garden Murder Case, The (novel)
    Garden Murder Case, The (1936) MGM

Gracie Allen Murder Case, The (novel)
    Gracie Allen Murder Case, The (1939) PAR

Greene Murder Case, The (novel)
    Greene Murder Case, The (1929) PAR
    Night of Mystery (1937) PAR

Kennel Murder Case, The (novel)
    Kennel Murder Case, The (1933) WB
    Calling Philo Vance (1940) WB

VAN DRUTEN, JOHN

After All (play)
    New Morals for Old (1932) MGM

Behold, We Live (play)
    If I Were Free (1934) RKO

Bell, Book and Candle (play)
    Bell, Book and Candle (1958) COL

Diversion (play)
    Careless Age, The (1929) FN

I Remember Mama (play based on K. Forbes's novel)
    I Remember Mama (1948) RKO

Old Acquaintance (play)
    Old Acquaintance (1943) WB
    Rich and Famous (1981) MGM/UA

There's Always Juliet (play)
    One Night in Lisbon (1941) PAR

Voice of the Turtle, The (play)
    Voice of the Turtle, The (1947) WB

VAN LOON, WILLEM HENDRICK

Story of Mankind, The (nonfiction)
    Story of Mankind, The (1957) WB

VANCE, ETHEL

Escape (novel)
    Escape (1940) MGM

Winter Meeting (novel)
        Winter Meeting (1948) WB

VANCE, LOUIS JOSEPH

Alias the Lone Wolf (novel)
        Alias the Lone Wolf (1927) COL

First Cabin (story)
        Cheaters at Play (1932) F

Joan Thursday (novel)
        Greater Than Marriage (1925) VIT

Lone Wolf, The (novel)
        Lone Wolf, The (1924) AE

Main Spring (story)
        Lost at Sea (1926) TIF

Mrs. Paramour (novel)
        Married Flirts (1924) MG

VANE, SUTTON

Outward Bound (play)
        Outward Bound (1930) WB
        Between Two Worlds (1944) WB
        Flight That Disappeared, The (1961) UA

VEILLER, BAYARD

Chatterbox, The (play)
        Smooth as Satin (1925) FBO
        Alias French Gertie (1930) RKO

Danger (story)
        Woman With Four Faces, The (1923) PAR

Thirteenth Chair, The (play)
        Thirteenth Chair, The (1919) PAT
        Thirteenth Chair, The (1929) MGM
        Thirteenth Chair, The (1936) MGM

Trial of Mary Dugan, The (play)

Trial of Mary Dugan, The (1929) MGM
Trial of Mary Dugan, The (1941) MGM

Within the Law (play)
    Within the Law (1917) VIT
    Within the Law (1922) FN
    Paid (1930) MGM
    Within the Law (1939) MGM

VERNE, JULES

Around the World in 80 Days (novel)
    Around the World in 80 Days (1956) UA

Captain Grant's Children (novel)
    In Search of the Castaways (1962) BV

Career of a Comet (novel)
    Valley of the Dragons (1961) COL

Five Weeks in a Balloon (novel)
    Five Weeks in a Balloon (1962) TCF

From the Earth to the Moon (novel)
    From the Earth to the Moon (1958) WB

Journey to the Center of the Earth (novel)
    Journey to the Center of the Earth (1959) TCF

Light at the Edge of the World, The (novel)
    Light at the Edge of the World, The (1971) NG

Master of the World (novel)
    Master of the World (1961) AI

Mathais Sandorf (novel)
    Isle of Zorda (1922) PAT

Michael Strogoff (novel)
    Michael Strogoff (1926) U
    Soldier and the Lady, The (1937) RKO

Mysterious Island, The (novel)
    Mysterious Island, The (1929) MGM
    Mysterious Island, The (1961) COL

Robur, the Conqueror (novel)

        Master of the World (1961) AI

Southern Star, The (novel)
        Southern Star, The (1969) COL

Twenty Thousand Leagues Under the Sea (novel)
        Twenty Thousand Leagues Under the Sea (1916) U
        Twenty Thousand Leagues Under the Sea (1954)
        BV

VIDAL, GORE

Best Man, The (play)
        Best Man, The (1964) UA

Myra Breckenridge (novel)
        Myra Breckenridge (1970) TCF

Visit to a Small Planet (play)
        Visit to a Small Planet (1960) PAR

VIGNY, BENNO

Amy Jolly (play)
        Morocco (1930) PAR

VONNEGUT, JR., KURT

Happy Birthday, Wanda June (play)
        Happy Birthday, Wanda June (1971) COL

Slaughterhouse-Five (novel)
        Slaughterhouse-Five (1972) U

W

WAKEFIELD, DAN

Starting Over (novel)
    Starting Over (1979) PAR

WALLACE, EDGAR

Dangerous to Know (play)
    Dangerous to Know (1938) PAR

Dark Eyes of London, The (novel)
    Human Monster, The (1940) MON

Death Watch (novel)
    Before Dawn (1933) RKO

Feathered Serpent, The (novel)
    Menace, The (1932) COL

Four Just Men (novel)
    Secret Four, The (1940) MON

Ghost of John Holling (novel)
    Mystery Liner (1934) MON

Greek Poropulis, The (story)
    Born to Gamble (1935) REP

Ringer, The (story)
    Phantom Strikes, The (1939) MON

Sanders of the River (novel)
    Coast of Skeletons (1965) SA

Squeakers, The (story)
    Murder on Diamond Row (1937) UA

Terror, The (play)
    Terror, The (1928) WB

WALLACE, FRANCIS

Kid Galahad (novel)
    Kid Galahad (1937) WB
    Kid Galahad (1962) UA

Stadium (story)
    Touchdown! (1931) PAR

WALLACE, IRVING

Chapman Report, The (novel)
    Chapman Report, The (1962) WB

Man, The (novel)
    Man, The (1972) PAR

Prize, The (novel)
    Prize, The (1964) MGM

WALLACE, LEW

Ben-Hur (novel)
    Ben-Hur (1925) MGM
    Ben-Hur (1959) MGM

WALSH, MAURICE

Quiet Man, The (short story)
    Quiet Man, The (1952) REP

WALTER, EUGENE

Easiest Way, The (play)
    Easiest Way, The (1917) SEZ
    Easiest Way, The (1931) MGM

Just a Woman (play)
    Just a Woman (1925) FN
    No Other Woman (1933) RKO

Nancy Lee (play)
    Way of a Woman, The (1919) SE

Trail of the Lonesome Pine, The (play from J. Fox's novel)
    Trail of the Lonesome Pine, The (1916) PAR
    Trail of the Lonesome Pine, The (1923) PAR
    Trail of the Lonesome Pine, The (1936) PAR

WAMBAUGH, JOSEPH

Black Marble, The (novel)
    Black Marble, The (1980) AVCO

New Centurions, The (novel)
    New Centurions, The (1972) COL

Onion Field, The (novel)
    Onion Field, The (1979) AVCO

WARREN, ROBERT PENN

All the King's Men (novel)
    All the King's Men (1949) COL

Band of Angels (novel)
    Band of Angels (1957) WB

WATTERS, GEORGE MANKER

Burlesque (play)
    Dance of Life (1929) PAR
    Swing High, Swing Low (1937) PAR
    When My Baby Smiles at Me (1948) TCF

WAUGH, EVELYN

Loved One, The (novel)
    Loved One, The (1965) MGM

WEAD, FRANK

Ceiling Zero (play)
    Ceiling Zero (1935) WB

Lady With a Braid (story in collab. Ferdinand
Reyher)
    Stranded (1935) WB

WEBB, CHARLES

Graduate, The (novel)
    Graduate, The (1967) EMB

Marriage of a Young Stockbroker, The (novel)
    Marriage of a Young Stockbroker, The (1971)
    TCF

WEBSTER, JEAN

Daddy Long Legs (novel, play)
    Daddy Long Legs (1919) FN
    Daddy Long Legs (1931) F
    Daddy Long Legs (1955) TCF

WELLMAN, PAUL I.

Broncho Apache (novel)
    Apache (1954) UA

Iron Mistress, The (novel)
    Iron Mistress, The (1952) WB

Jubal Troop (novel)
    Jubal (1956) COL

Walls of Jericho, The (novel)
    Walls of Jericho, The (1948) TCF

WELLS, H.G.

Empire of the Ants (short story)
    Empire of the Ants (1977) AI

First Men in the Moon (novel)
    First Men in the Moon (1964) COL

Food of the Gods, The (novel)
    Village of the Giants (1965) EMB
    Food of the Gods, The (1976) AI

Invisible Man, The (novel)
    Invisible Man, The (1933) U

Island of Dr. Moreau, The (novel)
    Island of Lost Souls (1933) PAR
    Island of Dr. Moreau, The (1977) AI

Kipps (novel)
    Remarkable Mr. Kipps, The (1942) TCF
    Half a Sixpence (1968) PAR

Time Machine, The (novel)
    Time Machine, The (1960) MGM

War of the Worlds, The (novel)
    War of the Worlds, The (1953) PAR

White Unicorn, The (story)
    One Woman's Story (1949) U

WERFEL, FRANZ

Jacobowsky and the Colonel (play in collab. S.N.
Behrman)
    Me and the Colonel (1958) COL

Juarez and Maximilian (play)
    Juarez (1939) WB

Phantom Crown, The (play based on Bertita Harding's
novel)
    Juarez (1939) WB

Song of Bernadette, The (novel)
    Song of Bernadette, The (1944) TCF

WEST, MAE

Diamond Lil (play)
    She Done Him Wrong (1933) PAR

WEST, MORRIS L.

Salamander, The (novel)
    Salamander, The (1983) ITC

Shoes of the Fisherman, The (novel)
    Shoes of the Fisherman, The (1968) MGM

WEST, NATHANAEL

Day of the Locust, The (novel)
    Day of the Locust, The (1975) PAR

Miss Lonelyhearts (novel)
    Advice to the Lovelorn (1933) TCF
    Lonelyhearts (1959) UA

WESTON, GEORGE

Jem of the Old Rock (novel)
    Winning Girl (1919) PAR

Kingdom of Heart's Desire (novel)
    You Never Saw Such a Girl (1919) PAR

Salt of the Earth (novel)
    Eyes of the Soul (1919) ARTCLASS

Village Cut-Up (story)
    Putting It Over (1919) PAR

WESTON, JOHN

Hail, Hero! (novel)
    Hail, Hero! (1969) CC

WEXLEY, JOHN

Last Mile, The (play)
    Last Mile, The (1932) WW
    Last Mile, The (1959) UA

WHARTON, EDITH

Age of Innocence, The (novel)
    Age of Innocence, The (1934) RKO

Children, The (novel)
    Marriage Playground, The (1929) PAR

Glimpses of the Moon (novel)
    Glimpses of the Moon (1923) PAR

Old Maid, The (novel)
    Old Maid, The (1939) WB

WHEELER, HARVEY

Fail-Safe (novel in collab. Eugene Burdick)
    Fail-Safe (1964) COL

WHITE, E.B.

Charlotte's Web (novel)
    Charlotte's Web (1973) PAR

WHITE, GRACE MILLER

Tess of the Storm Country (novel)
    Tess of the Storm Country (1914)
    Tess of the Storm Country (1922) UA
    Tess of the Storm Country (1932) F
    Tess of the Storm Country (1961) TCF

WHITE, LIONEL

Clean Break (novel)
    Killing, The (1956) UA

Money Trap, The (novel)
    Money Trap, The (1966) MGM

Snatchers, The (novel)

Night of the Following Day, The (1969) U

WHITE, STEWART EDWARD

Killer, The (novel)
    Mystery Ranch (1932) F

Two-Gun Man, The (story)
    Under a Texas Moon (1930) WB

Westerners, The (novel)
    Westerners, The (1919) HOD

Wild Geese Calling (novel)
    Wild Geese Calling (1941) TCF

WHITE, T.H.

Once and Future King, The (novel)
    Sword in the Stone, The (1963) BV
    Camelot (1967) WB/SA

WHITTIER, JOHN GREENLEAF

Barbara Frietchie (poem)
    Barbara Frietchie (1915) M
    Barbara Frietchie (1924) PDC

Barefoot Boy, The (poem)
    Barefoot Boy, The (1923) CBC
    Barefoot Boy, The (1938) MON

WIGGIN, KATE DOUGLAS

Mother Carey's Chickens (novel)
    Mother Carey's Chickens (1938) RKO
    Summer Magic (1963) BV

Rebecca of Sunnybrook Farm (play)
    Rebecca of Sunnybrook Farm (1917) PAR
    Rebecca of Sunnybrook Farm (1932) F
    Rebecca of Sunnybrook Farm (1938) TCF

Timothy's Quest (novel)

229

Timothy's Quest (1936) PAR

WILBUR, CRANE

Monster, The (play)
    Monster, The (1925) MG

Song Writer, The (story)
    Children of Pleasure (1930) MGM

WILDE, OSCAR

Canterville Ghost, The (story)
    Canterville Ghost, The (1944) MGM

Crime of Arthur Saville, The (short story)
    Flesh and Fantasy (1943) U

Lady Windermere's Fan (play)
    Lady Windermere's Fan (1919) TRI
    Lady Windermere's Fan (1925) WB
    Fan, The (1949) TCF

Picture of Dorian Gray, The (novel)
    Picture of Dorian Gray, The (1945) MGM

WILDER, ROBERT

And Ride a Tiger (novel)
    Stranger in My Arms (1959) U

Flamingo Road (novel)
    Flamingo Road (1949) WB

Fruit of the Poppy (novel)
    Sol Madrid (1968) MGM

Written on the Wind (novel)
    Written on the Wind (1957) U

WILDER, THORNTON

Bridge of San Luis Rey, The (novel)
    Bridge of San Luis Rey, The (1929) MGM

        Bridge of San Luis Rey, The (1944) UA

Matchmaker, The (play)
    Matchmaker, The (1958) PAR
    Hello, Dolly! (1969) TCF

Our Town (play)
    Our Town (1940) UA

WILLARD, JOHN

Cat and the Canary (play)
    Cat and the Canary (1927) U
    Cat Creeps, The (1930) U
    Cat and the Canary (1939) PAR

Fog (novel)
    Black Waters (1929) WOW

WILLIAMS, BEN AMES

All the Brothers Were Valiant (story)
    Across to Singapore (1928) MGM
    All the Brothers Were Valiant (1953) MGM

Barber John's Boy (story)
    Man to Man (1931) WB

Black Pawl (novel)
    Godless Men (1921) G

Leave Her to Heaven (novel)
    Leave Her to Heaven (1945) TCF

Prodigal's Mother (story)
    Someone to Remember (1943) REP

Small Town Girl (novel)
    Small Town Girl (1936) MGM

Son of Anak (story)
    Masked Emotions (1929) F

Strange Woman, The (novel)
    Strange Woman, The (1947) A

Toujours L'audace (story)
    Always Audacious (1920) PAR

WILLIAMS, EMLYN

Corn Is Green, The (play)
    Corn Is Green, The (1945) WB

Light of Heart (play)
    Life Begins at 8:30 (1942) TCF

Night Must Fall (play)
    Night Must Fall (1937) MGM

WILLIAMS, TENNESSEE

Cat on a Hot Tin Roof (play)
    Cat on a Hot Tin Roof (1958) MGM

Glass Menagerie, The (play)
    Glass Menagerie, The (1950) WB

Milk Train Doesn't Stop Here Anymore, The (play)
    Boom! (1968) U

Night of the Iguana, The (play)
    Night of the Iguana, The (1964) SA

Orpheus Descending (play)
    Fugitive Kind, The (1959) UA

Period of Adjustment (play)
    Period of Adjustment (1962) MGM

Roman Spring of Mrs. Stone, The (novel)
    Roman Spring of Mrs. Stone, The (1961) WB

Rose Tattoo, The (play)
    Rose Tattoo, The (1953) PAR

Seven Descents of Myrtle, The (play)
    Last of the Mobile Hot-Shots (1970) WB

Streetcar Named Desire, A (play)
    Streetcar Named Desire, A (1951) WB

Suddenly, Last Summer (play)
    Suddenly, Last Summer (1959) COL

Summer and Smoke (play)
    Summer and Smoke (1961) PAR

Sweet Bird of Youth (play)
    Sweet Bird of Youth (1962) MGM

This Property Is Condemned (play)
    This Property Is Condemned (1966) PAR

Twenty-Seven Wagons Full of Cotton (play)
    Baby Doll (1956) WB

WILSON, HARRY LEON

Cameo Kirby (play in collab. B. Tarkington)
    Cameo Kirby (1923) F
    Cameo Kirby (1930) F

His Majesty Bunker Bean (novel)
    His Majesty Bunker Bean (1918) PAR
    His Majesty Bunker Bean (1925) WB
    Bunker Bean (1936) RKO

Man From Home, The (play in collab. B. Tarkington)
    Man From Home, The (1922) PAR

Merton of the Movies (novel; play by Kaufman &
Connelly)
    Merton of the Movies (1924) PAR
    Make Me a Star (1932) PAR
    Merton of the Movies (1947) MGM

Oh, Doctor! (novel)
    Oh, Doctor! (1924) U
    Oh, Doctor! (1937) U

Ruggles of Red Gap (novel)
    Ruggles of Red Gap (1918) ES
    Ruggles of Red Gap (1923) PAR
    Ruggles of Red Gap (1935) PAR
    Fancy Pants (1950) PAR

WILSON, SLOAN

Man in the Gray Flannel Suit, The (novel)
    Man in the Gray Flannel Suit, The (1956) TCF

Summer Place, A (novel)
    Summer Place, A (1959) WB

WINSOR, KATHLEEN

Forever Amber (novel)
    Forever Amber (1947) TCF

WISTER, OWEN

Virginian, The (novel)
    Virginian, The (1914) PAR
    Virginian, The (1923) PAR
    Virginian, The (1929) PAR
    Virginian, The (1946) PAR

WODEHOUSE, P.G.

Anything Goes (play in collab. Guy Bolton)
    Anything Goes (1936) PAR
    Anything Goes (1956) PAR

Gentleman of Leisure, A (play in collab. John Stapleton)
    Gentleman of Leisure, A (1923) PAR

Piccadilly Jim (novel)
    Piccadilly Jim (1936) MGM

Thank You, Jeeves (story)
    Thank You, Jeeves (1936) TCF

Watch Dog, The (short story)
    Dizzy Dames (1936) LIB

WOLFE, TOM

Right Stuff, The (novel)
    Right Stuff, The (1983) WB

234

WOOD, MRS. HENRY

East Lynne (novel)
    East Lynne (1916) MT
    East Lynne (1921) HOD
    East Lynne (1925) F
    Ex-Flame (1930) TIF
    East Lynne (1931) F

WOODWARD, BOB

All the President's Men (nonfiction in collab. C. Bernstein)
    All the President's Men (1976) WB

WOOLLCOTT, ALEXANDER

Dark Tower, The (play in collab. G.S. Kaufman)
    Man With Two Faces, The (1934) FN

WOOLRICH, CORNELL

Black Curtain, The (story)
    Street of Chance (1942) PAR

Black Alibi (story)
    Leopard Man, The (1943) RKO

Cocaine (story)
    Fall Guy (1947) MON

Rear Window (short story)
    Rear Window (1954) PAR

WOUK, HERMAN

Caine Mutiny, The (novel)
    Caine Mutiny, The (1954) COL

Marjorie Morningstar (novel)
    Marjorie Morningstar (1958) WB

Slattery's Hurricane (novel)

        Slattery's Hurricane (1949) TCF

Youngblood Hawke (novel)
        Youngblood Hawke (1964) WB

WREN, PERCIVAL CHRISTOPHER

Beau Geste (novel)
        Beau Geste (1926) PAR
        Beau Geste (1939) PAR
        Beau Geste (1966) U

Beau Ideal (novel)
        Beau Ideal (1931) RKO

Beau Sabreur (novel)
        Beau Sabreur (1928) PAR

Wages of Virtue (novel)
        Wages of Virtue (1924) PAR

WRIGHT, HAROLD BELL

Calling of Dan Matthews, The (novel)
        Calling of Dan Matthews, The (1936) COL

Eyes of the World (story)
        Eyes of the World (1930) UA

Massacre River (novel)
        Massacre River (1949) AA

Mine With the Iron Door, The (story)
        Mine With the Iron Door, The (1936) COL

Recreation of Brian Kent, The (story)
        Wild Brian Kent (1926) RKO

Secret Valley (novel)
        Secret Valley (1937) TCF

Shepherd of the Hills, The (novel)
        Shepherd of the Hills, The (1919) WRI
        Shepherd of the Hills, The (1928) FN
        Shepherd of the Hills, The (1941) PAR

Son of His Father, A (story)
    Son of His Father, A (1917) PAR
    Son of His Father, A (1925) PAR

When a Man's a Man (novel)
    When a Man's a Man (1924) FN
    When a Man's a Man (1935) F

Winning of Barbara Worth, The (novel)
    Winning of Barbara Worth, The (1926) UA

WRIGHT, RICHARD

Native Son (novel)
    Native Son (1951) CLA

WRIGHT, S. FOWLER

Deluge, The (novel)
    Deluge, The (1933) RKO

WYLIE, I.A.R.

Gay Banditti, The (novel)
    Young at Heart, The (1938) UA

Grandma Bernie Learns Her Letters (story)
    Four Sons (1928) F

Hermit Doctor of Gaya (story)
    Stronger Than Death (1920) M

Inheritors, The (story)
    Gaiety Girl (1924) U

Jungle Law (story)
    Man Must Live (1925) PAR

Keeper of the Flame (novel)
    Keeper of the Flame (1943) MGM

Puritan at Large (story)
    Road to Reno, The (1938) U

Red Mirage (story)

Foreign Legion (1928) U

Vivacious Lady (story)
Vivacious Lady (1938) RKO

Widow's Evening (short story)
Evenings for Sale (1932) PAR

WYLIE, PHILIP

Gladiator, The (novel)
Gladiator, The (1938) COL

Night Unto Night (novel)
Night Unto Night (1949) WB

Pink Chemise (story)
Come On Marines (1934) PAR

Second Honeymoon (story)
Second Honeymoon (1937) TCF

When Worlds Collide (novel in collab. E. Balmer)
When Worlds Collide (1952) PAR

WYSS, JOHANN DAVID

Swiss Family Robinson (novel)
Swiss Family Robinson (1940) RKO
Swiss Family Robinson (1960) BV

X-Y-Z

XANROF, LEON

Prince Consort, The (play in collab. Jules Chanel)
    Love Parade, The (1929) PAR

YERBY, FRANK

Foxes of Harrow, The (novel)
    Foxes of Harrow, The (1947) TCF

Golden Hawk, The (novel)
    Golden Hawk, The (1952) COL

Saracen Blade, The (novel)
    Saracen Blade, The (1954) COL

YEZIERSKA, ANZIA

Hungry Hearts (short stories)
    Hungry Hearts (1922) G

Salome of the Tenements (novel)
    Salome of the Tenements (1925) PAR

YOUNG, MIRIAM

Mother Wore Tights (novel)
    Mother Wore Tights (1947) TCF

YOUNG, RIDA JOHNSON

Brown of Harvard (play)
    Brown of Harvard (1926) ES

Captain Kidd, Jr. (play)
    Captain Kidd, Jr. (1919) ART

Glorious Betsy (play)
    Glorious Betsy (1928) WB
    Hearts Divided (1936) WB

Little Old New York (play)
    Little Old New York (1940) TCF

Maytime (play)
    Maytime (1923) PRE
    Maytime (1937) MGM

Naughty Marietta (story)
    Naughty Marietta (1935) MGM

Out of the Night (story)
    Hell Harbor (1930) UA

YOUNG, STARK

So Red the Rose (novel)
    So Red the Rose (1935) PAR

YURICK, SOL

Warriors, The (novel)
    Warriors, The (1979) PAR

ZANGWILL, ISRAEL

Big Bow Mystery, The (play)
    Perfect Crime, The (1928) FBO
    Crime Doctor, The (1934) RKO
    Verdict, The (1946) WB

Merely Mary Ann (play)
    Merely Mary Ann (1931) F

Nurse Marjorie (novel)
    Nurse Marjorie (1920) REA

We Moderns (play)
    We Moderns (1925) FN

ZEIMER, GREGOR

Education for Death (nonfiction)
    Hitler's Children (1943) RKO

ZOLA, EMILE

Le Bete Humaine (novel)
    Human Desire (1954) COL

Nana (novel)
    Nana (1934) UA

Therese Raquin (novel)
    Shadows of Fear (1928) FN

ZWEIG, ARNOLD

Case of Sergeant Grischa, The (novel)
    Case of Sergeant Grischa, The (1930) RKO

INDEX

245

Bloodhounds of Broadway, 183
Bloodline, 195
Blue Bird, The, 144
Blue Blood, 127
Blue Blood and the Pirate, 126
Blue Denim, 99
Blue Eagle, 18
Blue Ribbon, The, 17
Bluebeard's Eighth Wife, 189
Bobby Deerfield, 177
Body and Soul, 211
Body Snatcher, The, 202
Bonjour Tristesse, 187
Bonne Chance, 86
Book of Carlotta, 21
Book of Daniel, The, 59
Boom!, 232
Boom Town, 82
Border Legion, The, 83
Borderland, 155
Born Reckless, 41
Born to Gamble, 222
Born to the West, 83
Born Yesterday, 116
Botany Bay, 90
Bottom of the Bottle, The, 198
Bought and Paid For, 26
Bound East for Cardiff, 162
Bound for Glory, 87
Boy and His Dog, A, 64
Boy Meets Girl, 201
Boy of Flanders, 56
Boy of Flanders, A, 165
Boy of Mine, 209
Boys in the Band, The, 50
Brand, The, 16
Brasher Doubloon, The, 38
Brave Cowboy, The, 1
Breach of Promise, 104
Bread on the Waters, 126
Breaking Point, The, 97
Breath of Scandal, A, 153

Murder at the Baskervilles, 60
Murder at the Vanities, 122
Murder for a Wanton, 38
Murder, My Sweet, 38
Murder of Dr. Harrigan, The, 63
Murder of Stephen Kester, The, 9
Murder on Diamond Row, 223
Murder on a Bridal Path, 166
Murder on a Honeymoon, 167
Murder on the Blackboard, 167
Murder on the Campus, 38
Murderers' Row, 90
Murders in the Rue Morgue, 170
Music Master, The, 124
Muss 'Em Up, 82
Mutiny on the Bounty, 90
My Best Girl, 159
My Blue Heaven, 131
My Brother Paul, 61
My Client Curley, 46
My Cousin Rachel, 61
My Darling Clementine, 129
My Fair Lady, 134
My Fair Lady, 193
My Foolish Heart, 187
My Forbidden Past, 13
My Four Years in Germany, 77
My Gal Sal, 61
My Life and Times, 213
My Man Godfrey, 93
My Old Man, 96
My Outlaw Brother, 26
My Own Pal, 18
My Wife and I, 205
Myra Breckenridge, 221
Mysterious Dr. Fu Manchu, The, 182
Mysterious Island, The, 220
Mysterious Mr. Wong, The, 119
Mystery House, 63
Mystery Liner, 222
Mystery of Edwin Drood, The, 58
Mystery of Huntings End, 63

301

307

317

What Every Woman Knows, 14
What Every Woman Knows, 74
What Happened to Jones?, 27
What Price Glory, 201
What Price Glory, 7
Wheel of Chance, 107
Wheels of Fate, 52
When a Man Loves, 172
When a Man's a Man, 237
When Knighthood Was in Flower, 145
When Ladies Meet, 50
When My Baby Smiles at Me, 224
When Romance Rides, 86
When Strangers Meet, 74
When the Legends Die, 25
When Tomorrow Comes, 32
When Worlds Collide, 12
When Worlds Collide, 238
When You Comin' Back, Red Ryder?, 150
Where Eagles Dare, 143
Where Is the Tropic of Capricorn?, 44
Where Love Has Gone, 181
Where Sinners Meet, 153
Where the Pavement Ends, 185
Where's Charlie?, 212
While Satan Sleeps, 127
While the Patient Slept, 63
Whipped, The, 178
Whistling in the Dark, 35
White and Yellow, 138
White Angel, The, 205
White Banners, 59
White Buffalo, The, 187
White Cargo, 81
White Circle, The, 203
White Cliffs, The, 152
White Cliffs of Dover, The, 152
White Cockatoo, The, 63
White Dawn, The, 103
White Fang, 138
White Lady, 71
White Monkey, The 75